THE REVELATION OF JESUS CHRIST

TRANSLATION — COMMENTARY — PERSONAL EXPERIENCES

BY DR. DONALD A. PEART

The Revelation of Jesus Christ –Translation- Commentary-
Personal Experiences ©2015 Donald Peart

ISBN-13: 978-1523666614

ISBN-10: 1523666617

Cover Design: Jeshua Peart

First Edition: January 2016
Current Edition: March 2024

COMMENTS

It is with joy I greet you who have decided to read this book concerning the Revelation of Jesus Christ. The first section of this volume consists of the book of Revelation with some words (**in bold text**) that is the Greek transliteration of those words, followed by a second section consisting of my brief commentary on portions of the book of Revelation, and finally a third section consisting of some personal revelations my wife, Judith and I experienced through our Lord Jesus Christ.

With that said, I would also like to note since I really like the style of the King James and the fact that it is classified as "public domain," I have used that translation as a base for this book with transliteration of some of the Greek words from the Majority text (the Byzantine texts); and I have also cited the Alexandrian text. With regard to the verses in this volume, I have excluded the *cursive* words that were added in the King James Version; however, they were not in the Greek texts.

I pray that the Holy Spirit of Wisdom and Revelation rest upon you that the eyes of your heart may be enlightened with spiritual understanding, even as you read this book. May the grace of our Lord Jesus Christ, the love of God, the Father and the communion of the Holy Spirit be with your spirit, soul, and body!

Kindly,
Donald Peart

TABLE OF CONTENTS

PREFACE

In the summer of 1981, about a year after I graduated from Baltimore Polytechnic High School, by providence my wife (at that time, we were dating) and I decided to read the Bible. I remember reading the book of John first, and eventually I ended up reading the entire book of Revelation after reading a track. After reading the entire book of Revelation, the words of Jesus came to pass in my life concerning the book of Revelation.

"Blessed is he that **reads,** and they that **hear** the words of this prophecy...." —Revelation 1:3a.

I became blessed in that my then girlfriend (now my wife of 29 ½ years) and I dedicated our lives to the Lord Jesus that day; albeit I lasted for all of two weeks. I had no one to teach me and I did not know anything about finding a Church. It would be five years later, while on my second tour in the USMC, that I would commit to the Lord Jesus fully, and my wife also. This commitment to the Lord Jesus Christ is a direct result of reading the book of the Revelation of Jesus Christ.

With that said, after I read the book of Revelation in 1981, for some reason Revelation 20:4 was intriguing to me. I remember questioning a particular portion of the verse asking, "What does it mean when the verse says, 'souls' will be raised from the dead?" I had no concept of what the "soul" is! It was this verse (Revelation 20:4) that the Lord Jesus used to place a hunger in me to seek to understand Jesus, Himself, the Revelation of Jesus Christ and of course Revelation 20:4.

After Judy and I rededicated our lives to Jesus Christ in April (the Passover season) of 1986, I eventually committed myself to seeking the Spirit of the Lord Jesus for answers from/in the book of Revelation, especially, the understanding of what it

i

means for "souls" to be raised from the dead. I became committed to having and finding answers from the book of the Revelation of Jesus Christ. Why?

Jesus and the angels said that it was an open book to His Church (Revelation22:10). The Revelation of Jesus Christ also says, **"Behold, I come quickly; blessed is he who keeps the sayings of the prophecy of this book"** (Revelation 22:7). It is a blessing to keep the sayings of the book of the Revelation of Jesus Christ, so in order for us to keep the sayings, we must be able to understand the sayings of the book of The Revelation of Jesus Christ.

The book of the Revelation of Jesus Christ is also written for the Church made up of Jews and Gentiles. It was not written just for the Jews, and it was not written just for the Gentiles. The Revelation of Jesus Christ is written for the Churches of Jesus Christ. "I Jesus have sent mine angel to testify unto you these things in **the churches"** (Revelation 22:16).

As indicated in Revelation 1:3: May you read — know again — the prophecy of the book of the Revelation of Jesus Christ. May you hear and understand the prophecy of the book of the Revelation of Jesus Christ! May you keep — guard with the eyes — the words that are written in the Revelation of Jesus Christ.

May the Lord Jesus be revered, who is blessed forever more!

THE REVELATION OF JESUS CHRIST
CHAPTER 1

1 Revelation of Jesus Christ, which God gave to him, to show to his **servants** things which must **swiftly become**; and he sent and signified through his angel to his servant John.

2 Who bare record of the Word of God, and of the testimony of Jesus Christ, and of all things that he saw.

3 Blessed is he that **knows-again,** and they that hear the words of this prophecy, and keep those things which are written therein, because the **season squeezes.**

4 John to the seven churches which are in Asia; Grace to you, and peace, from him who is, and who was, and who **is-coming;** and from the seven Spirits which are before his throne.

5 And from Jesus Christ, the **Believing** witness, the **Firstborn** of the dead, and the Prince of the kings of the earth. To him **who loves** us, and washed us from our sins in his own blood,

6 And has made us **a kingdom**, priests to God and his Father; to him glory and dominion forever and ever. Amen.

7 Be-perceiving, he **is-coming** with clouds; and every eye shall see him, and they which pierced him; and all kindred of the earth shall **be-grieve-struck** because of him. Even so, amen!

8 I am Alpha and Omega, says the Lord **God**, who is, and who was, and who **is-coming**, the Almighty.

9 I John, who also am your brother, and **co-participant** in tribulation, and in the kingdom and **endurance** of Jesus Christ, was in the island that is called Patmos, for the Word of God, and for the testimony of Jesus Christ.

10 I **became in** the Spirit **in** the Lord's Day, and heard behind me a mega voice, as of a trumpet.

11 Saying, I am Alpha and Omega, the First and the Last; and, what you see, write in a book, and send to the seven churches; to Ephesus, and to Smyrna, and to Pergamos, and to Thyatira, and to Sardis, and to Philadelphia, and to Laodicea.

12 And I turned to see the voice that spoke with me. And being turned, I saw seven golden candlesticks.

13 And in the **middle** of the seven candlesticks like to the Son of man, clothed with a garment down to the foot, and **girded** about the **breast** with a golden **pocket-belt**.

14 His head and hairs white like wool, as white as snow; and his eyes as a flame of fire.

15 And his feet like to **copper-incense**, as if they burned in a furnace, and his voice as the sound of many waters.

16 And he had in his right hand seven stars; and out of his mouth went a sharp two-edged sword; and his countenance as the sun shines in his **power.**

17 And when I-**perceived** him, I fell at his feet as dead. And he laid his right hand upon me, saying to me, fear not; I am the First and the Last.

18 And the living-one, and was dead; and, **be-perceiving**, I am alive **into the ages of the ages**, amen; and have the keys of Hell and of Death.

19 Write the things which **you-perceived**, and the things which are, and the things **intending is-becoming after these**.

20 The **secret** of the seven stars which you saw in my right hand, and the seven golden candlesticks. The seven stars are the angels of the seven churches; and the seven candlesticks which you saw are the seven churches.

CHAPTER 2

1 To the angel of the church of Ephesus write, these things say he that holds the seven stars in his right hand, who walks in the **middle** of the seven golden candlesticks.

2 I-**perceived** your **acts,** and your **fatigue,** and your **endurance,** and how you cannot bear them which are **bad**; and you have tried them which say they are apostles, and are not, and have found them **false**.

3 And has **lifted**, and has **endured,** and through my name has **fatigued,** and has not **wearied.**

4 Nevertheless, I have against you, because you have left your first love.

5 Remember therefore from **which-place** you are fallen, and **change-mind**, and do the first works; or else I will come to you **swiftly,** and will remove your candlestick out of his place, except you **change-mind.**

6 But this you have, that you hate the acts of the Nicolaitans, which I also hate.

7 He that has an ear let him hear what the Spirit says to the churches; **to-the one-conquering** will I give to eat of the tree of life, which is in the **middle** of the paradise of God.

8 And to the angel of the church in Smyrna write, these things say the First and the Last, which was dead, and is alive.

9 I know your **acts,** and tribulation, and **beggary,** (but you are rich); and the blasphemy of them which say they are Jews, and are not, but the synagogue of Satan.

10 Fear none of those things which **you-are-intending emotion**; behold, the devil shall cast **out-of** you into prison, that you may be tried; and you shall have tribulation ten days; be you **believing** to death, and I will give you a crown of life.

11 He that has an ear let him hear what the Spirit says to the churches; **the one-conquering** shall not be hurt of the second death.

12 And to the angel of the church in Pergamos write these things say he which has the sharp sword with two-edges.

13 I know your works, and where you dwell, where Satan's **throne** and you hold fast my name, and have not denied my faith, even in those days wherein Antipas my **believing** martyr, who was slain among you, where Satan dwells.

14 But I have a few things against you, because you have them there that hold the doctrine of Balaam, who taught Balak to cast a stumbling block before the children of Israel, to eat things sacrificed to idols, and to **prostitute**.

15 So have you also them that hold the doctrine of the Nicolaitans, which thing I hate.

16 Change-mind; or else **I-am-coming** to you **swiftly** and will fight against them with the sword of my mouth.

17 He that has an ear, let him hear what the Spirit says to the churches; **to-the one-conquering** will I give to eat of the hidden manna, and will give him a white stone, and in the stone a new name written, which no man knows except he who receives.

18 And to the angel of the church in Thyatira write, these things say the Son of God, who has his eyes like to a flame of fire, and his feet like **copper-incense**.

19 I know your **acts**, and love, and service, and faith, and your **endurance**, and your **acts**; and the last more than the first.

20 Notwithstanding I **have against you, that** you **tolerate your wife Jezebel,** which calls herself a prophetess, **and** teach and **cause-to-stray** my servants to **prostitution** and to eat **image-sacrifices.**

21 And I gave her time to change-her-mind; and she does not want change-her-mind of her prostitution.

22 Behold, I will cast her into a bed, and them that commit adultery with her into **mega** tribulation, except they **change-mind out-of** their **acts.**

23 And I will kill her children with death; and all the churches shall know that I am he who searches the **kidneys** and hearts; and I will give to every one of you according to your **acts**.

24 But to you I say, and to the rest in Thyatira, as many as have not this doctrine, and which have not known the depths of Satan, as they speak; I will put upon you none other burden.

25 But that which you have, **you-hold** until I **arrive**.

26 And **the one-conquering,** and keeps my **acts** to the **finish**, to him will I give **authority** over the nations.

27 And he shall **shepherd** them with a rod of iron; as the vessels of a potter shall they be **together-crushed;** even as I received of my Father.

28 And I will give him the morning star.

29 He that has an ear let him hear what the Spirit says to the churches.

CHAPTER 3

1 And to the angel of the church in Sardis write these things says he that has the seven Spirits of God, and the seven stars; I know your acts, that you have a name that you live and are dead.

2 Be watchful, and **stand-fast** the things which remain, that are **intending** to die; for I have not found your **acts filled** before **my** God.

3 Remember therefore how you have received and heard, and **guard**, and **change-mind**. If therefore you shall not watch, I **shall-arrive** on you as a thief, and you shall not know what hour I will **arrive** upon you.

4 Nevertheless you have a few names in Sardis which have not **soiled** their garments; and they shall walk with me in white; for they are worthy.

5 The one-conquering, the same shall be clothed in white **garment**; and I will not blot out his name out of the Book of Life, but I will confess his name before my Father, and before his angels.

6 He that has an ear let him hear what the Spirit says to the churches.

7 And to the angel of the church in Philadelphia write these things says he that is holy, he that is true, he that has the **locker** of David, he that opens, and no man **locks;** except he that opens, and no man shall open.

8 I **perceived** your **acts; be-perceiving,** I have set before you an open door, and no man can **lock** it; for you have a little strength, and have **guard** my Word, and has not denied my name.

9 Behold, I will make them of the synagogue of Satan, which say they are Jews, and are not, but **are-falsifying;** behold, I will make them **arrive** and worship before your feet, and to know that I have loved you.

10 Because you have **guarded** the Word of my **endurance,** I also will **guard** you **out-of** the hour of temptation, which **intending is-coming** upon all the **occupied-houses,** to try them that dwell upon the earth.

11 Be-perceiving, I come **swiftly;** hold that fast which you have, that no man takes your crown.

12 The one-conquering will I make a pillar in the temple of my God, and he shall go no more out; and I will write upon him the name of my God, and the name of the city of my God, new Jerusalem, which **is-descending** out of heaven from my God; and my new name.

13 He that has an ear let him hear what the Spirit says to the churches.

14 And to the angel of the church of the Laodiceans write; these things say the Amen, the **Believing** and True Witness, the Beginning of the creation of God.

15 I know your works, that you are neither cold nor hot; **you-owe** to be cold or hot.

16 So then because you are warm and neither cold nor hot, **I-am-intending to-vomit** you out of my mouth.

17 Because you say, I am rich, and increased with goods, and have need of nothing; and **perceive** not that you are **talent-tested**, and **mercy-able**, and **beggar**, and blind, and naked.

18 I counsel you to buy of me gold tried in the fire, that you may be rich; and white **garment**, that you may be clothed, and the **disfigure** of your nakedness do not appear; and **in-anoint** eyes with **plaster,** that you may see.

19 As many as I love, I **expose** and **discipline**; be zealous therefore, and **change-mind**.

20 Behold, I stand at the door, and knock; if any man hears my voice, and opens the door, I will come in to him, and will **dine** with him, and he with me.

21 The one-conquering will I grant to sit with me in my throne, even as I also overcame, and am set down with my Father in his throne!

22 He that has an ear let him hear what the Spirit says to the churches.

CHAPTER 4

1 After this I **perceived,** and behold, a door opened in heaven; and the first voice which I heard as it were of a trumpet talking with me; which said, **walk-up here,** and I will show you things which must be hereafter.

2 And immediately I was in **to-with-Spirit** and **perceived** a throne was **laid** in heaven, and **him-sitting** on the throne.

3 And he that **is-sitting** was to look upon like jasper and a sardine stone; and a rainbow round about the throne, like **seeing** an emerald.

4 And round about the throne twenty-four **thrones;** and upon the **thrones** I saw twenty-four elders sitting, clothed in white garment; and they had on their heads' crowns of gold.

5 And out of the throne **is-proceeding** lightnings and thunders and voices; and seven Lamps of fire burning before the thrones which are the seven Spirits of God.

6 And before the throne a sea of glass like **ice-frost** and in the middle of the throne, and round about the throne, four **living-things** full of eyes before and behind.

7 And the first **living-thing** like a lion, and the second **living-thing** like a calf, and the third **living-thing** had a face as a man, and the fourth **living-thing** like a flying eagle.

8 And the four **living-things** each of them, had six wings **around;** and full of eyes within; and they **up-pause** not day and night, saying, **holy, holy, holy, holy, holy, holy, holy, holy, holy Lord God Almighty,** who was, and is, and is to come.

9 And **whenever** those **living-things** give glory and honor and thanks **to-the one-sitting** on the throne, **to-the one-**living **into the ages of the ages.**

10 The twenty-four elders **sitting** on the throne fall down before him, and worship him that lives **into the ages of the ages**, and cast their crowns before the throne, saying:

11 You are worthy, **our Lord and God**, to receive glory and honor and power; for you have created all things, and **through** your **will** they **existed** and were created.

CHAPTER 5

1 And I saw in the **right** of **him-sitting** on the throne a book written inside and on the back, sealed with seven seals.

2 And I saw a **forceful** angel proclaiming with a **mega** voice, who is worthy to open the book, and to loose the seals thereof?

3 And no man in heaven, or in earth, neither under the earth, was able to open the book, neither to look **at-same.**

4 And I wept much, because no man was found worthy to open and to read the book, neither to look **at-same**.

5 And one of the elders says to me, weep not, **be-perceiving,** the Lion of the tribe of Judah, the Root of David, has **conquered** to open the book, and the seven seals thereof.

6 And I perceived and perceiving in the middle of the throne and of the four **living-things**, and in the middle of the elders, stood a Lamb as having-been-slain, having seven horns and seven eyes, which are the seven Spirits of God sent forth into all the earth.

7 And he came and took the book out of the right of him **sitting** upon the throne.

8 And when he had taken the book, the four **living-things** and twenty-four elders fell down before the Lamb, having every one of them harps, and golden **bowls** full of **incense**, which are the prayers of saints.

9 And they **are-singing** a new song, saying, you are worthy to take the book, and to open the seals thereof; for you were slain, and have redeemed us to God **in** your blood **out-of** every kindred, and tongue, and people, and nation.

10 And have made **them** to our God **a kingdom** and priests; and **they** shall reign on the earth.

11 And I beheld, and I heard the voice of many angels round about the throne and the **living-things** and the elders; and the number of them was ten thousand, times ten **thousand,** and thousands of thousands.

12 Saying with a loud voice, worthy is the Lamb that was slain to receive power, and riches, and wisdom, and strength, and honor, and glory, and blessing.

13 And every creature which is in heaven, and on the earth, and under the earth, and such as are in the sea, and all that are in them, I heard saying, blessing, and honor, and glory, and power, to him that sits upon the throne, and to the Lamb **forever and ever. Amen.**

14 And the four **living-things** said, amen. And the elders **fell** and worshipped.

CHAPTER 6

1 And I saw when the Lamb opened one of the **seven** seals, and I heard, as it were the noise of thunder, one of the four **living-things** saying, come and look.

2 And **I-perceived and be-perceiving** a white horse and he sitting on him had a bow; and a crown was given to him; and he went forth conquering, and to conquer.

3 And when he had opened the second seal, I heard the second **living-thing** say, come.

4 And there went out another **horse of fire** and **it-was-given** to **him-sitting** on him to take peace from the earth, and that they should kill one another; and there was given to him a mega **battle-knife.**

5 And when he had opened the third seal, I heard the third **living-thing** say, Come and **look.** And **I-perceived** and **be-perceiving** a black horse; and **he-sitting** on him had a **yoke** in his hand.

6 And I heard a voice in the middle of the four **living-thing** say, a measure of wheat for a **denarius**, and three measures of barley for a **denarius**; and the oil and the wine not **you-should-hurt.**

7 And when he had opened the fourth seal, I heard the voice of the fourth **living-thing** say, come and **look.**

8 And **I-perceived** and **be-perceiving** a **greenish** horse; and his name that **sitting** on him was Death and Hell followed with him. And **authority** was given to them over the fourth part of the earth, to kill with sword, and with hunger, and with death, and **under** the **beasts** of the earth.

9 And when he had opened the fifth seal, **I-perceived** under the sacrifice-place the souls of them that were slain for the Word of God, and for the testimony which they held.

10 And they cried with a mega voice, saying, how long, **the Owner**, holy and true, do you not judge and avenge our blood on them that dwell on the earth?

11 And white robes were given to every one of them; and it was said to them, that they should **pause** yet for a **micro time**, until their fellow servants also and their brethren **are-intending** be killed as they, should be fulfilled.

12 And **I-perceived** when he had opened the sixth seal and **be-perceiving** there was a mega earthquake; and the sun became black as sackcloth of hair, and the moon became as blood.

13 And the stars of heaven fell to the earth, even as a fig tree cast her **unripe** figs, when she is shaken of a **mega** wind.

14 And the heaven departed as a scroll when it is **coiled**; and every mountain and island were moved out of their places.

15 And the kings of the earth, and the **mega great-men**, and the **rich-men**, and the **chief-of thousands**, and the **powerful-men**, and every **slave**, and every **free-man**, hid themselves in the dens and in the rocks of the mountains.

16 And said to the mountains and rocks, fall on us, and hide us from the face of **him-sitting** on the throne, and from the **grasping-anger** of the Lamb.

17 For the **mega** day of his **grasping-anger** is come; and who shall be able to stand?

CHAPTER 7

1 And after these things **I-perceived** four angels standing on the four corners of the earth, holding the four winds of the earth, that the wind should not blow on the earth, nor on the sea, nor on any tree.

2 And I saw another angel ascending from **rising of-sun**, having the seal of the living God; and he cried with a mega voice to the four angels, to whom it was given to hurt the earth and the sea,

3 Saying, hurt not the earth, neither the sea, nor the trees, until we have sealed the servants of our God in their foreheads.

4 And I heard the number of them which were sealed; a hundred forty-four thousand sealed **out-of** all the tribes of the children of Israel.

5 Out-of the tribe of Judah sealed twelve thousand. **Out-of** the tribe of Reuben sealed twelve thousand. **Out-of** the tribe of Gad sealed twelve thousand.

6 Out-of the tribe of Asher sealed twelve thousand. **Out-of** the tribe of Naphtali sealed twelve thousand. **Out-of** the tribe of Manasseh sealed twelve thousand.

7 Out-of the tribe of Simeon sealed twelve thousand. **Out-of** the tribe of Levi sealed twelve thousand. **Out-of** the tribe of Issachar sealed twelve thousand.

8 Out-of the tribe of Zebulon sealed twelve thousand. **Out-of** the tribe of Joseph sealed twelve thousand. **Out-of** the tribe of Benjamin sealed twelve thousand.

9 After this **I-perceived**, and, **be-perceiving** a **much** multitude, which no man could number, of all nations, and kindred, and people, and tongues, stood before the throne, and before the Lamb, clothed with white robes, and palms in their hands.

10 And cried with a mega voice, saying, salvation to our God which sits upon the throne, and to the Lamb.

11 And all the angels stood round about the throne, and the elders and the four **living-things**, and fell before the throne on their faces, and worshipped God,

12 Saying, amen! The blessing, and the glory, and the wisdom, and the thanksgiving, and the honor, and the power, and the **forcefulness** to our God into the ages of ages, amen!

13 And one of the elders answered, saying to me, what are these which are arrayed in white robes, and where came they?

14 And I said to him, **my Lord,** you **perceived**. And he said to me, these are they which **are-coming** out of **the mega** tribulation, and have washed their robes, and made them white in the blood of the Lamb.

15 Therefore are they before the throne of God and serve him day and night in his temple; and he **that-is-sitting** on the throne shall **tent** among them.

16 They shall hunger no more, neither thirst anymore; neither shall the sun **fall** on them, nor any heat.

17 For the Lamb which is in the middle of the throne shall **shepherd** them and shall lead them **to fountains of waters of life;** and God shall wipe away all tears from their eyes.

CHAPTER 8

1 And when he had opened the seventh seal, there was **hush** in heaven **as** half an hour.

2 And I saw the seven angels which stood before God; and to them were given seven trumpets.

3 And another angel came and stood at the altar, having **golden frankincense**; and there was given to him much incense, that he should **give to-the** prayers of all saints upon the golden **sacrifice-place** which was before the throne.

4 And the **smoke** of the incense **to-the** the prayers of the saints, ascended up before God out of the angel's hand.

5 And the angel took the **frankincense**, and filled it with fire of the altar, and cast into the earth; and there were voices, and thunders, and lightnings, and an earthquake.

6 And the seven angels who had the seven trumpets **internally-prepared** themselves to **trumpet**.

7 The first angel **trumpeted**, and there followed hail and fire **mixed** with blood, and they were cast upon the earth; **a third of the earth was burned-down,** and the third of trees was **burned-down**, and all green grass was **burned-down**.

8 And the second angel **trumpeted**, and as it were a **mega** mountain burning with fire was cast into the sea; and the third of the sea became blood.

9 And the third part of the creatures which were in the sea, **having soul,** died and the third of the ships were **through-rotted.**

10 And the third angel **trumpeted**, and there fell a **mega** star from heaven, burning as it were a lamp, and it fell upon the third of the rivers, and upon the fountains of waters.

11 And the name of the star is called **Absinth**; and the third of the waters became **absinth;** and many men died of the waters, because they were made **bitter.**

12 And the fourth angel **trumpeted**, and the third of the sun was **pounded**, and the third of the moon, and the third of the stars; so, as the third of them was **obscured**, and the day not **may-be-lighten** for a third of it, and the night **like-as.**

13 And **I-perceived**, and heard an **eagle** flying **in** the **midheaven,** saying with a loud voice, Woe, woe, woe, to the **dwellers** of the earth by reason of the **remaining** voices of the trumpet of the three angels, **of-is-intending to-be-trumpeting!**

CHAPTER 9

1 And the fifth angel **trumpeted**, and **I-perceived** a star fall from heaven **into** the earth; and to him was given the **locker** of the **well of-the abyss.**

2 And he opened the **well of-the abyss**; and there arose a smoke out of the pit, as the smoke of a **mega** furnace; and the sun and the air were **obscured** by reason of the smoke of the pit.

3 And there came out of the smoke locusts upon the earth; and to them was given **authority**, as the scorpions of the earth have **authority**.

4 And it was commanded them that they should not hurt the grass of the earth, neither any green thing, neither any tree; but only those men which have not the seal of God on their foreheads.

5 And to them it was given that they should not kill them, but that they should be tormented five months; and their torment as the torment of a scorpion, when he strikes a man.

6 And in those days shall men seek death and shall not find it; and shall desire to die, and death shall flee from them.

7 And the shapes of the locusts like to horses **internally-prepared** to battle; and on their heads as it were crowns like gold, and their faces as the faces of men.

8 And they had hair as the hair of women, and their teeth were as of lions.

9 And they had **chest**, as it were **chest** of iron; and the sound of their wings as the sound of chariots of many horses running to battle.

10 And they had tails like to scorpions, and there were stings in their tails; and their **authority** to hurt men five months.

11 And they had a king over them, the angel of the **abyss**, whose name in the Hebrew tongue, Abaddon, but in the Greek tongue has a name, Apollyon.

12 One woe is past; **be-perceiving, are-come** two woes more **after these**.

13 And the sixth angel **trumpeted,** and I heard a voice from the four horns of the golden **sacrifice-place,** which is before God,

14 Saying to the sixth angel which had the trumpet, loose the four angels which are bound in the **mega** river Euphrates.

15 And the four angels were loosed, which were **internally-prepared** for an hour, and a day, and a month and a year, for to slay the third of men.

16 And the number of the army of the horsemen **ten-thousands of-ten-thousands**, and I heard the number of them.

17 And **in-this-way I-perceived** the horses in the vision, and **them-sitting** on them, having **chest** of fire, and of **hyacinth**, and **God-sulfur-lightning-like;** and the heads of the horses as the heads of lions; and out of their mouths issued fire and smoke and **God-sulfur-lightning**.

18 By these three was the third of men killed, by the fire, and by the smoke, and by the **God-sulfur-lightning**, which issued out of their mouths.

19 For **the authority of the horses** in their mouth, and in their tails; for their tails like to serpents, and had heads, and with them they do hurt.

20 And the rest of the men which were not killed by these plagues yet not **they-changed-mind** of the **acts** of their hands, that they should not worship devils, and idols of gold, and silver, and brass, and stone, and of wood, which neither can see, nor hear, nor walk;

21 Neither **they-repented out-of** their murders, nor **out-of** their **drugs-potion**, nor **out-of** their **prostitution**, nor **out-of** their thefts.

CHAPTER 10

1 And **I-perceived** another **forcible** angel come down from heaven, clothed with a cloud; and a rainbow upon his head, and his face as the sun, and his feet as pillars of fire.

2 And he had in his hand a **booklet** open; and he set his right foot upon the sea and left on the earth.

3 And cried with a loud voice, as a lion roars; and when he had cried, seven thunders uttered their voices.

4 And when the seven thunders had **spoken** their voices, **I-was intending** to write; and I heard a voice from heaven saying to me, seal up those things which the seven thunders **spoke**, and write them not.

5 And the angel which I saw stand upon the sea and upon the earth lifted his **right** hand to heaven.

6 And swore by him that lives forever and ever, who created heaven, and the things that therein are, and the earth, and the things that are **in her**, and the sea, and the things which are **in her**, that there should be time no longer.

7 But in the days of the voice of the seventh angel, **whenever he-is-intending trumpeting,** the secrct of God **was-finished,** as he has **evangelized** to his servants the prophets.

8 And the voice which I heard from heaven spoke to me again, and said, go take the **booklet** which is open in the hand of the angel which stands upon the sea and upon the earth.

9 And I went to the angel, and said to him, give me the **booklet**. And he said to me, take and eat it up; and it shall make your belly bitter, but it shall be in your mouth sweet as honey.

10 And I took the **book** out of the angel's hand and ate it; and it was in my mouth sweet as honey; and as soon as I had eaten it, my belly was bitter.

11 And **they** said to me, you must prophesy again on many peoples, and nations, and tongues, and kings.

CHAPTER 11

1 And there was given me a reed likened to a rod saying, rise and measure the temple of God, and the altar, and **them-worshiping in it**.

2 But the court which is **outside** the temple **you-cast-out outside and** measure **her** not; for it is given to the Gentiles; and the holy city shall they tread under foot forty-two months.

3 And I will **give** to my two witnesses, and **they shall prophesy** a thousand two hundred **sixty** days, clothed in sackcloth.

4 These are the two olive trees, and the two candlesticks standing before the **Lord** of the earth.

5 And if any man will hurt them, **fire proceeds out of their mouth,** and devours their enemies; and if any man will hurt them, he must in this manner be killed.

6 These have **authority** to **lock** heaven that it rains not in the days of their prophecy; and have **authority** on waters to turn them to blood, and to smite the earth with all plagues, **as-many-times if-ever**.

7 And when they shall have finished **the testimony**, the beast that 'is ascending' out of **the abyss** shall make war against them, and shall overcome them, and kill them.

8 And their **fall** in the street of the mega city, which spiritually is called Sodom and Egypt, **wherever** also **their** Lord was crucified.

9 And they of the people and kindred and tongues and nations see their **fall** three days and a half and shall not **forgive** their **fall** to be put in graves.

10 And they that dwell upon the earth shall rejoice over them, and make merry, and shall send gifts one to another; because these two prophets tormented them that dwelt on the earth.

11 And after three days and a half the Spirit of life from God entered into them, and they stood upon their feet; and **mega** fear fell upon them which saw them.

12 And they heard a mega voice from heaven saying to them, **walk-up here.** And they **walked-up** to heaven in a cloud; and their enemies **looked-closely-at** them.

13 And **in that hour** was there a **mega** earthquake, and the tenth of the city fell and in the earthquake were **killed names of-men** seven thousand; and the remnant was **in-fear** and gave glory to the God of heaven.

14 The second woe is past; **be-perceiving** the third woe **is-coming shortly.**

15 And the seventh angel **trumpeted;** and there were mega voices in heaven, saying, the **kingdom** of this world **became of-our** Lord, and of his Christ; and he shall reign **into the ages of ages.**

16 And the twenty-four elders, **the-ones sitting** before God on their **thrones,** fell upon their faces, and worshipped God,

17 Saying, we give you thanks, O Lord God Almighty, **which are, and was;** because you have taken to you your **mega** power and have reigned.

18 And the nations were **grasping-angry,** and your **grasping-anger** is come, and the season of the dead, that they should be judged, and that you should give reward to your servants the prophets, and to the saints, and them that fear your name, small and **mega**; and should **through-rotted** them which **through-rotting** the earth.

19 And the temple of God was opened in heaven, and there was seen in his temple the Ark **the Covenant His Covenant**; and there were lightnings, and voices, and thunders, and an earthquake, and **mega** hail.

CHAPTER 12

1 And there appeared a **mega** wonder in heaven; a woman clothed with the sun and the moon under her feet and upon her head a crown of twelve stars.

2 And she **in belly holding** cried, travailing in birth, and **tormented to-produce**.

3 And there appeared another wonder in heaven; and behold a **mega fiery-red** dragon, having seven heads and ten horns, and seven crowns upon his heads.

4 And his tail **dragged** the third of the stars of heaven and did cast them to the earth; and the dragon stood before the woman **who-of-intending to-produce, to-eat-down** her child **whenever she-produced**.

5 And she **produced a son, a male, who is-intending** to shepherd all nations with a rod of iron; and her child **is-snatched towards** God, and his throne.

6 And the woman fled into the wilderness, where she has a place **internally-prepared from** God that **they-should-nourish** her there a thousand two hundred sixty days.

7 And there was war in heaven; Michael and his angels fought against the dragon; and the dragon fought and his angels.

8 And **not they-are-forceful**; neither was **a place for him** found any more in heaven.

9 And the **mega** dragon was cast out, that **original** serpent, called the Devil, and Satan, which **cause-to stray** the **whole habitable-house**; he was cast out into the earth, and his angels were cast out with him.

10 And I heard a **mega** voice saying in heaven, now is come salvation, and **power,** and the kingdom of our God, and the **authority** of his Christ; for the **categorizer** of our brethren is cast down, which **categorized** them before our God day and night.

11 And they overcame him by the blood of the Lamb and by the word of their testimony; and they loved not their **souls until** death.

12 Therefore, rejoice you heavens, and you that **tabernacle** in them. Woe to the **dwellers** of the earth and of the sea! For the devil is come down to you, having **mega sacrifice-wrath**, because he **perceives** that he has but a **puny** time.

13 And when the dragon saw that he was cast to the earth, he persecuted the woman **any-who produced the male.**

14 And to the woman were given two wings of a **mega** eagle that she might fly into the wilderness, into her place, where she is nourished for a **season**, and **seasons**, and half a **season** from the face of the serpent.

15 And the serpent cast out of his mouth water as a flood after the woman, that he might cause her to be **river-burdened**.

16 And the earth **ran-to the-cry of-the** woman, and the earth opened her mouth, and swallowed up the flood which the dragon cast out of his mouth.

17 And the dragon was **grasping-angry** with the woman and went to make war with the **remaining-ones** of her seed, which **guard** the commandments of God, and have the testimony of Jesus.

CHAPTER 13

1 And I stood upon the sand of the sea, and **perceived** a beast **walk-up** out of the sea, **having ten horns and seven heads**, and upon his horns ten crowns, and upon his heads the **names** of blasphemy.

2 And the beast which I saw was like to a leopard, and his feet were as of a bear, and his mouth as the mouth of a lion; and the dragon gave him his power, and his **throne**, and **mega** authority.

3 And **I-perceived first** of his heads as it were **butchered** to death; and his **plague of-the death** was **therapeutic**; and **marveled** the **whole earth behind** the beast.

4 And they worshipped the dragon which gave **authority** to the beast; and they worshipped the beast, saying, who like to the beast? Who is able to make war with him?

5 And there was given to him a mouth speaking **mega** things and blasphemies; and **authority** was given to him to **make-war** forty-two months.

6 And he opened his mouth in blasphemy against God, to blaspheme his name, and his tabernacle, them that **tabernacle** in heaven.

7 And it was given to him to make war with the saints, and to overcome them; and **authority** was given him over all kindred, **and people,** and tongues, and nations.

8 And all that dwell upon the earth shall worship him, whose names are not written in the Book of Life of the Lamb slain from the foundation of the world.

9 If any man has an ear, let him hear.

10 If anyone has captivity, he is going; if anyone in sword is-killing must himself in sword be-killed. Here is the **endurance** and the faith of the saints.

11 And **I-perceived** another beast **walking-up** out of the earth; and he had two horns like a lamb, and he spoke as a dragon.

12 And he **does** all the **authority** of the first beast before him and makes the earth and them which dwell **in her** to worship the **before-most** beast whose **plague of-death** was **therapeutic**.

13 And he does mega **signs**, so that he makes fire come down from heaven on the earth in the sight of men.

14 And **it-strays my-own-people** that dwell on the earth by those **signs** which **he-was-given** to do in the sight of the beast; saying to them that dwell on the earth, that they should make an image to the beast, which had the **plague** by a sword, and did live.

15 And **he was-given to-give spirit** to the image of the beast that the image of the beast should both speak and **make** as many as would not worship the image of the beast should be killed.

16 And he **makes** all, both small and **mega,** rich, and poor, free and bond, to **give themselves** an **engraving on** their **right,** or **on** their foreheads.

17 And that no man **may-be-able to-redeem** or sell, **if not the-one having** the **engraving,** the name of the beast, or the number of his name.

18 Here is wisdom. Let him that has understanding count the number of the beast; **it is the number because of a man**; and his number six-hundred sixty, six.

CHAPTER 14

1 And **I-perceived** and **be-perceiving 'the'** Lamb stood on the mount Zion, and with him a hundred forty-four thousand, having his name and his Father's name written on their foreheads.

2 And I heard a voice from heaven, as the voice of many waters, and as the voice of a **mega** thunder; and I heard the voice of harpers harping with their harps.

3 And **they-are-singing as a** new song before the throne, and before the four **living-things**, and the elders; and no man could **disciple** that song **if-not** the hundred forty-four thousand, which were redeemed from the earth.

4 These are they which were not **soiled** with women; for they are virgins. These are they which follow the Lamb whithersoever he goes. These were redeemed **by Jesus** from among **the** men, the first-fruit to God and to the Lamb.

5 And in their mouth was found no **falsehood**; for they are without fault.

6 And I saw another angel fly in the **mid-heaven**, having the everlasting gospel to **evangelize** them that dwell on the earth, and to every nation, and kindred, and tongue, and people,

7 Saying with a **mega** voice, fear God, and give glory to him; for the hour of his judgment is come; and worship him that made heaven, and earth, and the sea, and the fountains of waters.

8 And there followed another angel, saying, **Babylon the mega is fallen she has** made all nations drink of the wine of the **sacrifice-wrath** of her **prostitution**.

9 And the third angel followed them, saying with a **mega** voice, if any man worships the beast and his image, and **taking engraving on** his forehead, or **on** his hand.

10 The same shall drink of the wine of the **sacrifice-wrath** of God, which is **blended un-held** into the cup of his **grasping-anger**; and he shall be tormented with fire and **God-sulfur-lightning** in the presence of the holy angels, and in the presence of the Lamb.

11 And the smoke of their torment **walk-up into the ages of ages**; and they have no rest day or night, who worship the beast and his image, and whosoever **takes** the **engraving** of his name.

12 Here is the **endurance** of the saints **keeping** the commandments of God, and the faith of Jesus.

13 And I heard a voice from heaven saying to me, write, blessed the dead who die in the Lord from now; yes, says the Spirit that they may **up-pause** from their **weariness**; and their **acts** do follow them.

14 And **I-perceived**, and **be-perceiving** a white cloud, and upon the cloud **sitting** like to the Son of man, having on his head a golden crown, and in his hand a **keen gathering-hook**.

15 And another angel came out of the temple, crying with a mega voice to him **sitting** on the cloud, **send** in your **gathering-hook**, and reap; for the time is come to reap; for the harvest of the earth is **withered**.

16 And he **sitting** on the cloud **sends** in his **gathering-hook** on the earth; and the earth was reaped.

17 And another angel came out of the temple, which is in heaven, he also having a **keen gathering-hook**.

18 And another angel **out-came out-of** the altar, which had **authority** over fire; and cried with a loud cry to him that had the **keen gathering-hook**, saying, **send** in your **keen gathering-hook**, and gather the clusters of the vine of the earth; for her grapes are **pointed-ripe.**

19 And the angel **sends** in his **gathering-hook** into the earth, and gathered the vine of the earth, and cast into the **mega** winepress of the **sacrifice-wrath** of God.

20 And the winepress was trodden without the city, and blood came out of the winepress, **until** the horses' bridles, **from** a thousand six hundred **stadiums**.

CHAPTER 15

1 And **I-perceived** another sign in heaven, **mega** and marvelous, seven angels having the seven last plagues; for in them is filled up the **sacrifice-wrath** of God.

2 And I saw as it were a sea of glass **mixed** with fire; and them that **overcame out-of** the beast, and **out-of** his image and **out-of** the number of his name, stand on the sea of glass, having the harps of God.

3 And they sing the song of Moses the servant of God, and the song of the Lamb, saying, **mega** and marvelous your works, Lord God Almighty; just and true your ways, you King of **nations**.

4 Who shall not fear you, Lord, and glorify your name? For **only-you benign:** for all nations shall **arrive** and worship before you; for your **righteousness** are made manifest.

5 And after that **I-perceived**, and, **be-perceiving,** the temple of the tabernacle of the testimony in heaven was opened.

6 And the seven angels came out of the temple, having the seven plagues, clothed in pure and white linen, and having their **chest belted** with golden **pocket-belt**.

7 And one of the four **living-things** gave to the seven angels, seven golden **bowls** full of the **sacrifice-wrath** of God, who lives **into the ages of ages**.

8 And the temple was filled with smoke from the glory of God, and from his power; and no man was able to enter into the temple, until the seven plagues of the seven angels were **finished**.

CHAPTER 16

1 And I heard a mega voice out of the temple saying to the seven angels, Go your ways, and pour out the **seven bowls** of the **sacrifice-wrath** of God **into** the earth.

2 And the first went and poured out his **bowl upon** the earth; and **became bad** and **hurtful ulcers into** the men which had the **engraving** of the beast and them which worshipped his image.

3 And the second angel poured out his **bowl into** the sea; and it became as the blood of a **dead-one** and every living soul died in the sea.

4 And the third angel poured out his **bowl** upon the rivers and fountains of waters; and they became blood.

5 And I heard the angel of the waters say, you are righteous, who are, and was, and **the benign**, because you have judged these.

6 For they have shed the blood of saints and prophets, and you have given them blood to drink; for they are worthy.

7 And I heard the sacrifice-place say, even so, Lord God Almighty, true, and righteous your judgments.

8 And the fourth angel poured out his **bowl** upon the sun; and **it-was-given** to him to scorch men with fire.

9 And men were scorched with mega heat, and blasphemed the name of God, which has **authority** over these plagues; and they not **they-change-mind** to give him glory.

10 And the fifth angel poured out his **bowl** upon the **throne** of the beast; and his kingdom was full of darkness; and they chewed their tongues for pain.

11 And blasphemed the God of heaven, because of their pains and their ulcers, and not **they-changed-mind out-of** their **acts**.

12 And the sixth angel poured out his **bowl** upon the **mega** river Euphrates; and the water thereof was dried up, that the way of the kings of the **rising sun** might be **internally-prepared**.

13 And **I-perceived** three unclean spirits like frogs out of the mouth of the dragon, and out of the mouth of the beast, and out of the mouth of the false prophet.

14 For they are the spirits of devils, **making signs** go forth to the kings of the whole **habitable-house,** to gather them to the battle of **that day, the mega,** of God **the** Almighty.

15 Be-perceiving, I-am-coming as a thief. Blessed *is* he that watches, and **guard** his garments, lest he walk naked, and they **look-at** his **disfigurement.**

16 And he gathered them together into a place called in the Hebrew tongue **Armageddon**.

17 And the seventh angel poured out his **bowl** into the air; and there came a **mega** voice out of the temple of heaven, from the throne, saying, **it-has-become.**

18 And there were voices, and thunders, and lightnings; and there was a **mega** earthquake, such as was not since men were upon the earth, an earthquake **such-as-this,** so **mega.**

19 And the **mega** city was divided into three parts, and the cities of the nations' fell; and mega Babylon came in remembrance before God, to give to her the cup of the wine of the **sacrifice-wrath of-the** his **grasping-anger**.

20 And every island fled away, and the mountains were not found.

21 And there fell upon men a **mega** hail out of heaven, talent-like; and men blasphemed God because of the plague of the hail; for the plague thereof was **mega, vehemently-violent**.

CHAPTER 17

1 And there came one of the seven angels which had the seven bowls, and talked with me, saying to me, come here; I will show to you the judgment of the mega **female-prostitute** that sits upon many waters.

2 With whom the kings of the earth have **prostituted**, and the **dwellers** of the earth have been made drunk with the wine of her **prostitution**.

3 So he carried me away in the spirit into the wilderness; and **I-perceived** a woman sit upon a scarlet colored beast, full of names of blasphemy, having seven heads and ten horns.

4 And the woman was arrayed in purple and scarlet color, and **gilded** with gold and precious stones and pearls, having a golden cup in her hand full of **stink** and **un-cleansed** of her **prostitution of the earth**.

5 And upon her forehead a name written, **secret, Babylon, the mega, the mother of female-prostitutes and stinks** of the earth.

6 And **I-perceived** the woman drunken with the blood of the saints, and with the blood of the martyrs of Jesus; and when **I-perceived** her, I **marveled** with mega **marvel**.

7 And the angel said to me, why did you marvel? I will tell you the **secret** of the woman, and of the beast that carries her, which has the seven heads and ten horns.

8 The beast that you saw was and is not; and **is-intending to-be-ascending out-of** the **abyss** and go into perdition; and they that dwell on the earth shall **marvel**, whose names were not written in the Book of Life from the foundation of the world, when they **look-at** the beast that was, and is not, and **shall-be-present**.

9 And here the mind which has wisdom. The seven heads are seven mountains, on which the woman **is-sitting**.

10 And there are seven kings; five are fallen, and one is, the other is not yet come; and **whenever** he comes, he must **remain puny**.

11 And the beast that was, and is not, even he is the eighth, and is **out-of** the seven, and goes into perdition.

12 And the ten horns which **you-perceived** are ten kings, which have received no kingdom as yet; but receive **authority** as kings **first** hour with the beast.

13 These have **first opinion** and shall **give-throughout** their **authority** and **power** to the beast.

14 These shall make war with the Lamb, and the Lamb shall overcome them; for he is Lord of lords, and King of kings; and they that are with him called, and chosen, and **believing**.

15 And he says to me, the waters which **you-perceived**, where the **female-prostitute is-sitting**, are peoples, and multitudes, and nations, and tongues.

16 And the ten horns which you saw **and** the beast; these shall hate the **female-prostitute**, and shall make her desolate and naked, and shall eat her flesh, and burn her with fire.

17 For God **give into** their hearts to **do the opinion of him**, and to **do first opinion**, and give their kingdom to the beast, until the **declarations** of God shall be **finished**.

18 And the woman which **you-perceived is the city, the mega, having a kingdom** over the kings of the earth.

CHAPTER 18

1 And after these things I saw another angel come down from heaven, having **mega authority**; and the earth was **illuminated out-of** his glory.

2 And he cried with a **mega** voice, saying, Babylon the **mega** is fallen, is fallen, and is become the **dwelling** of demons, and the **guard-place** of every unclean spirit, and a **guard-place** of every unclean and hateful bird.

3 For all nations have drunk of the wine of the **sacrifice-wrath** of her **prostitution,** and the kings of the earth have **prostituted** with her, and the merchants of the earth are waxed rich through the **power** of her **straining**.

4 And I heard another voice from heaven, saying, come out of her, my people, that you be not partakers of her sins, and that you receive not of her plagues.

5 For her sins have reached to heaven, and God has remembered her iniquities.

6 Reward her even as she rewarded, and double to her double according to her works. In the cup which she has filled fill to her double.

7 How much she has glorified herself, and lived **straining,** so much torment and sorrow give her; for she says in her heart, I sit a queen, and am no widow, and shall see no sorrow.

8 Therefore shall her plagues **arrive** in **first** day, death, and mourning, and famine; and she shall be utterly burned with fire; for **forcible** the Lord God who **has judged** her.

9 And the kings of the earth, **prostitute with her** and lived **straining** with her, shall bewail her, and lament for her, when they shall see the smoke of her burning.

10 Standing afar off for the fear of her torment, saying, **woe, woe**, that **mega** city Babylon, that **forcible** city! For in **first** hour is your judgment come.

11 And the merchants of the earth shall weep and mourn over her; for no man buys their merchandise any more.

12 The merchandise of gold, and silver, and precious stones, and of pearls, and fine linen, and purple, and silk, and scarlet, and all **fragrant** wood, and all manner vessels of ivory, and all manner vessels of most precious wood, and of brass, and iron, and marble,

13 And cinnamon, and odors, and ointments, and frankincense, and wine, and oil, and fine flour, and wheat, and **domestic-animals**, and sheep, and horses, and chariots, and **bodies**, and souls of men.

14 And the fruits that your soul lusted after are departed from you and all things which were **fat** and **radiant** are departed from you, and you shall **not-still** find them.

15 The merchants of these things, which were made rich by her, shall stand afar off for the fear of her torment, **sobbing** and wailing,

16 And saying, **woe, woe,** that **mega** city, that was clothed in fine linen, and purple, and scarlet, and **gilded** with gold, and precious stones, and pearls!

17 For in **first** hour **so-much** riches are come to nothing. And every **navigator**, and all the company **of** ships, and sailors, and as many as trade by sea, stood afar off,

18 And cried when they saw the smoke of her burning, saying, what like to this **mega** city!

19 And they cast dust on their heads, and cried, weeping, and wailing, saying, **woe, woe,** that **mega** city, wherein were made rich all that had **floaters** in the sea by reason of her **expensiveness**! For in **first** hour is she made desolate!

20 Rejoice over her, the heaven, **and the saints, and the** apostles and **the** prophets; for God has **judged your judgment out-of** her.

21 And a **forcible** angel took up a stone like a **mega** millstone, and cast into the sea, saying, thus with violence shall that **mega** city Babylon be thrown down, and shall **not-still** be found.

22 And the voice of harpers, and musicians, and of pipers, and trumpeters, shall be heard no more at all in you; and no craftsman, of whatsoever craft, shall be found any more in you; and the sound of a millstone shall be heard no more at all in you.

23 And the light of a candle shall shine no more at all in you; and the voice of the bridegroom and of the bride shall be heard no more at all in you; for your merchants were the **mega** men of the earth; for by your **drugs** were all nations **strayed**.

24 And in her was found the blood of prophets, and of saints, and of all that were slain upon the earth.

CHAPTER 19

1 And after these things I heard **something like** a **mega** voice of much people in heaven, saying, alleluia, salvation, and glory, and honor, and power, to the Lord our God.

2 For true and righteous his judgments; for he has judged the **mega female-prostitute,** which did **rot** the earth **in** her **prostitution**, and has avenged the blood of his servants at her hand.

3 And again they said, alleluia; and her smoke **is-ascending into the ages of ages.**

4 And the twenty-four elders and the four **living-things** fell down and worshipped God that **is-sitting** on the throne, saying, amen; alleluia.

5 And a voice came out of the throne, saying, praise our God, all you his servants, and you that fear him, both small and **mega**.

6 And I heard as it were the voice of a **much** multitude, and as the voice of **much water** and as the voice of **forcible** thunders, saying, alleluia, for the Lord God omnipotent reigns.

7 Let us be glad and rejoice and give honor to him; for the marriage of the Lamb is come and his wife has made herself **internally-prepared**.

8 And to her was granted that she should be arrayed in fine linen, clean and white; for the fine linen is the **righteousness-acts** of saints.

9 And he says to me, write: Blessed **the-ones** which are called to the marriage **dinner** of the Lamb. And he says to me, these are the true sayings of God.

10 And I fell at his feet to worship him. And he said to me, **stare** you not, I am your fellow servant, and of your brethren that have the testimony of Jesus, worship God; for the testimony of Jesus is the spirit of prophecy.

11 And **I-perceived** heaven opened and behold a white horse; and he **sitting** upon him called **Believing** and True, and in righteousness he doth judge and make war.

12 His eyes as a flame of fire, and on his head many crowns; and he has names written and a name written, that no man knew, **if not him**.

13 And he **was-clothed** with vesture dipped in blood; and his name is called The Word of God.

14 And the armies in heaven followed him upon white horses, clothed in **pure white linen.**

15 And out of his mouth goes a sharp **two-edged** sword, that with it he should smite the nations; and he shall **shepherd** them with a rod of iron; and he treads the winepress of the **sacrifice-wrath and grasping-anger** of Almighty God.

16 And he has on vesture and on his thigh a name written, King of kings, and Lord of lords.

17 And I saw **one** angel standing in the sun; and he cried with a **mega** voice, saying to all the fowls that fly in **mid-heaven**, come, and gather yourselves together to the **mega supper of the God**.

18 That you may eat the flesh of kings, and the flesh of captains, and the flesh of **forcible** men, and the flesh of horses, and of them that sit on them, and the flesh of all, free and slaves, both small and **mega**.

19 And I saw the beast, and the kings of the earth, and their armies, gathered together to make war against him that sat on the horse, and against his army.

20 And the beast was taken, and with him the false prophet that wrought signs before him, with which he deceived them that had received the **engraving** of the beast, and them that worshipped his image. These both were cast alive into a lake of fire burning with **God-sulfur-lightning.**

21 And the **remaining-ones** were slain with the sword which proceeded out of his mouth of him **sitting** upon the horse; and all the fowls were filled with their flesh.

CHAPTER 20

1 And **I-perceived** an angel come down from heaven, having the key of the bottomless pit and a **mega** chain in his hand.

2 And he **use-vigor** on the dragon, that **original** serpent, which is the Devil, and Satan, and bound him a thousand years.

3 And cast him into the **abyss**, and **lock him**, and **seal up-above** him, that he should not still **stray** the nations, **until** the thousand years **finished**; and after these he must be loosed a **small time**.

4 And I saw thrones, and they **seated** upon them, and judgment was given to them; and the souls of them that were beheaded through the witness of Jesus, and through the Word of God, and **any-who** had not worshipped the beast, neither his image, neither had **taken the engraving** on their foreheads, or on their hands; and they lived and **kings** with Christ **'the'** thousand years.

5 But the rest of the dead lived not again until the thousand years were finished. This is the first resurrection.

6 Blessed and holy he that has **course** in the first resurrection; on such the second death has no **authority**, but they shall be priests of God and of Christ and **shall-be-kings** with him a thousand years.

7 And when the thousand years are **finished**, Satan shall be loosed out of his prison.

8 And shall go out to **stray** the nations which are in the four quarters of the earth, Gog, and Magog, to gather them together to battle; the number of whom as the sand of the sea.

9 And they went up on the breadth of the earth, and compassed the camp of the saints about, and the beloved city; and fire came down from God out of heaven and devoured them.

10 And the devil that **strayed** them was cast into the lake of fire and **God-sulfur-lighting,** where **also** the beast and the false prophet, and shall be tormented day and night **into the ages of the ages**.

11 And **I-perceived** a mega white throne, and him that sat on it, from whose face the earth and the heaven fled away; and there was found no place for them.

12 And **I-perceived** the dead, small and **mega**, stand before **the throne**; and the books were opened; and another book was opened, which is of life; and the dead were judged out of those things which were written in the books, according to their **acts**.

13 And the sea gave up the dead which were in **her;** and Death and Hell **gave** up the dead which were in them; and they were judged **each** according to their acts.

14 And Heath and Hell were cast into the lake of fire. This is the second death, **the lake of fire.**

15 And **if-any** was not found written in the Book of Life was cast into the lake of fire.

CHAPTER 21

1 And **I-perceived** a new heaven and a new earth; for the first heaven and the first earth were passed away; and there was no more sea.

2 And **I perceived** the holy city, New Jerusalem, coming down from God out of heaven, **internally-prepared** as a bride adorned for her husband.

3 And I heard a mega voice out of heaven saying, **be-perceiving,** the tabernacle of God with men, and he will dwell with them, and they shall be his people, and God himself shall be with them, their God.

4 And God shall wipe away all tears from their eyes; and there shall be no more death, neither sorrow, nor crying, neither shall there be any more pain; for the **before-most** things are **gone-from**.

5 And he **sitting** on the throne said, **be-perceiving**, I make all things new. And he said to me, write; for these words are true and **believing**.

6 And he said to me, **it-has-become.** I am Alpha and Omega, the **Beginning,** and the **Finish.** I will give to him that is athirst of the fountain of the water of life freely.

7 He that overcomes **I shall give him these things**; and I will be his God, and **he shall be to me the Son.**

8 But the **timid,** and unbelieving, and the **stink,** and murderers, and **male-prostitutes**, and **druggists,** and **image-servants**, and all **falsifiers**, shall have their **course** in the lake which burns with fire and **God-sulfur-lightning** which is the second death.

9 And there came one of the seven angels which had the seven bowls full of the seven last plagues, and talked with me, saying, come here, I will show you **the woman, the Lamb's bride.**

10 And he carried me away in the **Spirit** to a **mega** and high mountain, and showed me the **holy City, Jerusalem,** descending out of heaven from God.

11 Having the glory of God; and her light like to a stone precious, even like a jasper stone, **crystallized.**

12 And had a wall, mega and high, **having** twelve gates, and at the gates twelve angels, and names written thereon, which are of the twelve tribes of the children of Israel.

13 On the east three gates; on the north three gates; on the south three gates; and on the west three gates.

14 And the wall of the city had twelve foundations, and in them the **twelve** names of the twelve apostles of the Lamb.

15 And he that talked with me had a golden reed to measure the city, and the gates **of-her**, and the wall **of-her.**

16 And the city lays **four-cornered**, and the length is as much as the breadth; and he measured the city with the reed, twelve thousand **stadiums**. The length and the breadth and the height of it are **equal.**

17 And he measured the wall thereof, a hundred forty four cubits, the measure of a man, that is, of the angel.

18 And the **in-building** of the wall of it was jasper; and the city clean gold, like to **clean** glass.

19 And the foundations of the wall of the city **systemized** with all manner of precious stones. The first foundation jasper; the second, sapphire; the third, **copper-like**; the fourth, an emerald;

20 The fifth, **sardius-fingernail**; the sixth, sardius; the seventh, **gold-stone**; the eighth, beryl; the ninth, a topaz; the tenth, a **gold-leek**; the eleventh, a **hyacinth**; the twelfth, an **un-drunk.**

21 And the twelve gates twelve pearls; every gate was **out-of** one pearl; and the **plat** of the city was **clean** gold, **as** transparent glass.

22 And **I-perceived** no temple therein; for the Lord God Almighty and the Lamb is the temple **of-her.**

23 And the city had no need of the sun, neither of the moon, to shine; for the **very** glory of God did lighten it, and the Lamb the light **of-her.**

24 And the nations shall walk in the light **of-her**; and the kings of the earth do bring their glory and honor **of the nations to Him.**

25 And the gates of it shall not be **locked** at all by day; for there shall be no night there.

26 And they shall bring the glory and honor of the nations into **her that they may enter in.**

27 And there shall in no wise enter into it anything that defile, or **one-making stink, or falsehood;** but they which are written in the Lamb's Book of Life.

CHAPTER 22

1 And he showed me a river of water of life, **shining** as crystal, proceeding out of the throne of God and of the Lamb.

2 In the middle of the street of it, and on **both** side of the river, the tree of life, **making** twelve fruits, **giving** her fruit **one each** month; and the leaves of the tree for the **therapy** of the nations.

3 And there shall be no more **up-down**; but the throne of God and of the Lamb shall be in **her**; and his servants shall serve him.

4 And they shall see his face; and his name in their foreheads.

5 And there shall be no night there; and they need no candle, neither light of the sun; for the Lord God gives them light; and **they-shall-be kings into the ages of ages**.

6 And he said to me, these sayings **believing** and true; and the Lord God of the **spirits of** prophets sent his angel to show to his servants the things which must shortly be done.

7 Be-perceiving, I-am-coming swiftly blessed he that **guards** the sayings of the prophecy of this **booklet**.

8 And I John the one-who-hearing and the one-looking-at these things. And when I heard and saw, I fell down to worship before the feet of the angel which showed me these things.

9 Then says he to me, **stare not**; I am your fellow servant, and of your brethren the prophets and of them which **guard** the sayings of this **booklet**; worship God.

10 And he says to me, seal not the sayings of the prophecy of this **booklet**; for the **season is squeezing**.

11 He that is unjust, let him be unjust still; and he which is **soiled**, let him be **soiled** still; and he that **do right,** let him be **do right** still; and he that is holy, let him be holy still.

12 And, **be-perceiving, I-coming swiftly**; and my reward with me, to give every man according as his **acts** shall be.

13 I am the First and the Last, the Beginning and the Finish.

14 Blessed the **one-doing** his commandments that they may have **authority** to the tree of life and may enter in through the gates into the city.

15 Outside are-dogs, and **druggists**, and **male-prostitutes**, and murderers, and **image-servants**, and whosoever **friends** and makes **falsehood**.

16 I Jesus have sent mine angel to testify to you these things in the churches. I am the root and the offspring of David, the bright and morning star.

17 And the Spirit and the bride say, **come**. And let him that hears say, come. And let him that is **thirsty** come. And whosoever will, let him take the water of life freely.

18 For I testify to every man that hears the words of the prophecy of this **booklet,** if any man shall add to these things, God shall add to him the plagues that are written in this book.

19 And if any man shall take away from the words of the book of this prophecy, **may God take away** his **course** out of the **tree** of life, and out of the holy city, and the things which are written in this book.

20 He which testifies these things say, **yes, I-am-coming swiftly**. Amen. **Yes, be-you-coming,** Lord Jesus.

21 The grace of our Lord Jesus Christ with all **the saints**. Amen.

DONALD PEART COMENTARY
CHAPTER 1

1 Revelation of Jesus Christ,[1] which God gave to him, to show to his **servants** things which must **swiftly become**; and he sent and signified[2] through his angel to his servant John.

2 Who bare record of the Word of God, and of the testimony of Jesus Christ, and of all things that he saw.

3 Blessed is he that **knows-again,** and they that hear the words of this prophecy, and keep those things which are written therein; because the **season squeezes.**[3]

4 John to the seven churches which are in Asia; Grace to you, and peace, from him who is, and who was, and who **is-coming;** and from the seven Spirits[4] which are before his throne;

---

[1] Is this a facet of the Revelation of Jesus Christ that Paul mentioned in 1 Corinthians 1:7 which appears to be different from His coming in 1 Corinthians 1:8? This revelation of Jesus was given to Jesus after Jesus ascended to heaven. Jesus, in turn, assigned an angel to reveal the same to the beloved apostle John.

[2] To indicate by a mark or sign. Thus one of the ways to understand the book of Revelation is to ask the Holy Spirit to give you understanding about the many "signs" picture in the book of Revelation.

[3] That is, the present season squeezes "this prophecy;" or, time is "throttling" His prophecy; or prophecy and the season squeeze each other; or saying it yet another way, "this prophecy" of the book of Revelation is in its fulfillment mode of prophecy; it is no longer in future prophetic mode, but it is in fulfillment mode. Jesus said, the Law and the prophets prophesied until John. That is from the days of John, the Baptist until Jesus comes back the Scriptures are being fulfilled (Matthew 11:13; Ezekiel 12:21-28).

[4] 1. The Spirit of the Lord; 2. The Spirit of Wisdom; 3. The Spirit of Understanding, 4. The Spirit of Counsel; 5. The Spirit of Might; 6. The Spirit of Knowledge; 7. The Spirit of the Fear of the Lord (Isaiah 11:2).

5 And from Jesus Christ, the **Believing** witness, the **Firstborn**[5] of the dead, and the Prince of the kings of the earth. To him **who loves** us, and washed us from our sins in his own blood,

6 And has made us **a kingdom,**[6] **priests**[7] to God and his Father; to him glory and dominion forever and ever. Amen.

7 Be-perceiving, he **is-coming** with clouds;[8] and every eye shall see him, and they which pierced him; and all kindred of the earth shall **grieve-struck** because of him. Even so, amen!

8 I am Alpha and Omega, says the Lord **God**, who is, and who was, and who **is-coming**, the Almighty.

9 I John, who also am your brother, and **co-participant** in tribulation,[9] and in the kingdom and **endurance**[10] of Jesus Christ, was in the island that is called Patmos, for the Word of God, and for the testimony of Jesus Christ.

---

[5] The birthright belongs to Jesus and His "Church of the firstborns" (plural) mentioned in Hebrews 12:23. Yes, all of God's children have a birthright, which means that we inherit (tenant) all things that the Father has given to Jesus.

[6] The same phrase ("a kingdom and priests") used in Revelation 5:10 in reference to the four living ones and the twenty-four elders.

[7] The Church must remember that she is a royal priesthood of Jesus' Melchizedek order; and if that is understood, the book of Revelation is filled with the function of Jesus our Great-High Priest and His priests administering the priesthood, seen in pictures or signs like "the temple of God" the golden altar, the seven lampstands, priests in their linen garments with the belts, the Ark of the Covenant, God's Throne, the Mercyseat, and so on.

[8] Clouds can also be a symbol for people (Hebrews 12:1 in reference to all the clouds of people in Hebrews 11:1-40).

[9] Qualification to be counted worthy for the Kingdom of God (2 Thessalonians 1:4-7, Acts 14:22 w/Luke 20:35)

[10] The faith of Jesus that shows a willingness to die to keep the commandments of God rather than take the mark (engraving) of the beast (Revelation 13:10; 14:12).

10 I **became**[11] in the Spirit[12] **in** the Lord's Day,[13] and heard behind me a mega voice, as of a trumpet.[14]

11 Saying, I am Alpha and Omega, the First and the Last; and, what you see, write in a book, and send to the seven[15] churches; to Ephesus, and to Smyrna, and to Pergamos, and to Thyatira, and to Sardis, and to Philadelphia, and to Laodicea.

12 And I turned to see the voice[16] that spoke with me. And being turned, I saw **seven golden candlesticks.**[17]

13 And in the **middle**[18] of the seven candlesticks[19] like to the Son of man, clothed with a garment down to the foot, and **girded** about the **breast** with a golden **pocket-belt**.[20]

---

[11] This implies it was a gradual unveiling.

[12] "In the Spirit" is the same as being in heaven (Revelation 4:1-2).

[13] This is not referring to Sunday. This day of the Lord is the next Sabbath millennium, the Lord's day (see 2 Peter 3:8), the first six millenniums were man's days (judged by men); the next millennium with be the Lord's day (judged by Jesus and His saints both the resurrected saints and those who will still be living as part of the generations of that age.

[14] Jesus' voice is as a trumpet, always prophetic.

[15] These seven Churches are representative of the types of Churches that will exist in all generations of the ages.

[16] The voice of the Lord can be **seen** (Revelation 1:12-16), the voice of the Lord **walks** (Genesis 3:8)), the voice of the Beloved **knocks** (Song of Solomon 5:2).

[17] Note: Each Church is represented by a lampstand for a total of seven lampstands, and not one lampstand representing the seven Churches. Thus the function of all the fruits and gifts are to be represented in each respective local Church as seen in the bulbs, flowers, and almond fruits on the lampstand in Exodus.

[18] Christ in (the middle of) us, the hope of Glory (Colossians 1:27)

[19] See Revelation 1:20 and Revelation 11:3-4

[20] The belt is representative of Jesus' strength (Isaiah 22:21)

14 His head and hairs white[21] like wool,[22] as white as snow; and his eyes as a flame of fire.[23]

15 And his feet like to **copper-incense**,[24] as if they burned in a furnace; and his voice as the sound of many waters.

16 And he had in his right hand seven stars;[25] and out of his mouth went a sharp two-edged sword;[26] and his countenance as the sun shines in his **power.**[27]

17 And when **I-perceived** him, I fell at his feet as dead.[28] And he laid his right hand upon me, saying to me, fear not; I am the First and the Last.

18 And the living-one, and was dead; and, **be-perceiving**, I am alive **into the ages of the ages**, amen; and have the keys of Hell[29] and of Death.[30]

---

[21] Purity that commands respect and glory (see Leviticus 19:32; Proverbs 16:31)

[22] The Ancient (lit., weaned) of Days

[23] Jesus' eyes of flames of fire have the ability to see the "end" results of people's action (see notes for Revelation 2:18).

[24] Jesus tempered judgments (copper) with prayer and intercession (incense)

[25] Seven stars represents the seven messengers of the Church in ever age (See Revelation 1:20). Thus, the other stars cited in the book of Revelation are also messengers of Jesus

[26] The "two-edged sword" is symbolic of God's Word ("logos" (spoken/written) and/or "rhema" (declarations) of God)—Hebrew 4:12, Ephesians 6:17.

[27] This is a concrete way to understand a facet of "power;" that is, the power of Jesus gives light and affects like the natural sun.

[28] People do sometimes fall out or fall down at the presence of the Lord—Matthew 28:4, Daniel 10:9, Acts 9:4, Ezekiel 1:28

[29] Jesus owns the keys of hell, included but not limited to the keys to her gates (Matthew 16:18).

[30] Jesus destroyed Satan who had the power of Death (Hebrews 2:14); and therefore, now Jesus holds the keys of Death and Hell that followed death.

19 Write the things which **you-perceived**, and the things which are, and the things **intending is-becoming after these.**

20 The **secret** of the seven stars which you saw in my right hand, and the **seven golden candlesticks**. The seven stars are the angels[31] of the seven churches; and the **seven candlesticks**[32] which you saw are the seven churches.

CHAPTER 2

1 To the angel of the church of Ephesus[33] write; these things say he[34] that holds the seven stars in his right hand, who walks in the **middle** of the seven golden candlesticks.

2 I-**perceived** your **acts,** and your **fatigue,** and your **endurance,** and how you cannot bear them which are **bad;** and you have tried them which say they are apostles, and are not, and have found them **false.**[35]

Christians are also passed from Death into life (John 5:24); death can no longer dominate us (Romans 6:9). It was not possible for Death to hold Jesus; God having loosed the pains of Death and raised Jesus from the dead (Acts 2:24).

[31] The angels also represent the corporate ministry of leaders of the Churches.

[32] The seven candlesticks (lampstands) represent the seven Churches of Jesus; and therefore, studying the candlestick built by Moses will give excellent insight with regards to the function of the Churches of Jesus in their respective locations.

[33] Ephesus is transliterated as: upon-within; which can point to the Father upon them and the Father within them (compare Ephesians 4:6).

[34] Jesus' specific introduction of certain traits of His to each angel of the Church usually shows His calling and/or purpose for the angel and Church (a principle learned from Thamo Naidoo of South Africa). In this case, the angel of the Church of Ephesus has a ministry to all seven stars (angels of the Church); that is, this messenger has a ministry to leaders; this angel also "walks" in an international capacity, demonstrated by Jesus walking in the middle of the seven golden candlesticks.

[35] False apostles do **not** function "in all '**bearing under to**-signs, **to**-wonders, and **to**-powers'" (2 Corinthians 12:12); false apostles boast in other men's measure (2

3 And has **lifted,** and has **endured,** and through my name has **fatigued,** and has not **wearied.**

4 Nevertheless, I have against you, because you have left your first love.

5 Remember therefore from **which-place** you are fallen, and **change-mind**, and do the first works; or else I will come to you **swiftly,** and will remove your candlestick out of his place, except you **change-mind.**

6 But this you have, that you hate the acts of the Nicolaitans,[36] which I also hate.

7 He that has an ear let him hear[37] what the Spirit says to the churches; **to-the one-conquering** will I give to eat[38] of the tree of life, which is in the **middle** of the paradise of God.[39]

Corinthians 10); false apostles always demand fees for preaching and boast in fleshly accomplishments and pedigree (2 Corinthians 11), etc.

[36] Conquer-laity; and this can relate to lording over God's flock (1 Peter 5:1-3).

[37] Faith comes by hearing preachers (Romans 10:14); hearing comes through the Word (declarations) of God (Romans 10:17); Faith also comes by God waking our ears to hear morning by morning (Isaiah 50:4-5). Sometimes our ears must be opened (lit., dug) in order for us to hear (Psalms 40:6). The more we "prick the ear" to hear, the more Jesus gives to us (Mark 4:23-25).

[38] This Church will be able to eat the fruit from the tree of life. The fruit of the tree of life is the flesh of Jesus Christ. In Genesis 3, the Hebrew word translated as "life" in the tree of life also means "raw (flesh)" according to Strong's dictionary. Jesus in John 6:53 indicated that we must eat His flesh; in Ezekiel 47:12 we learn that the fruit is the "firstborn" (Jesus). John 6:35 teaches that we must spiritually eat Jesus' flesh (come to Jesus) and spiritually drink Jesus' blood (believe into Jesus). See also the notes for Revelation 22:2. If God would have allowed Adam to eat from the tree of life (the raw flesh of Jesus), Adam would have lived "concealed" in his sinful state. The fact that God prevented Adam from eating from the tree of life shows the mercy of God towards Adam's redemption through Jesus.

[39] Paradise, where the tree of life exists, is also third heaven (1 Corinthians 12:1-4); since the tree of life exists in the Garden of Eden, the Garden of Eden is third

8 And to the angel[40] of the church in Smyrna[41] write; these things say the First and the Last, which was dead, and is alive. [42]

9 I know your **acts,** and tribulation,[43] and **beggary,** (but you are rich); and the blasphemy of them which say they are Jews,[44] and are not, but the synagogue[45] of Satan.

10 Fear none of those things which **you-are-intending emotion;**[46] behold, the devil shall cast out-of you into prison, that you may be tried; and you shall have tribulation ten days;

---

heaven. That is, Adam and Eve migrated between the Garden of Eden (third heaven) and the earth realm as the man in Paul's vision migrated (2 Corinthians 12:1-4); and as Jesus promised that this Church, Ephesus, would do if they overcome.

[40] Jesus' specific introduction of certain traits of His to each angel of the Church usually shows His calling and/or purpose for the angel and Church. In this case, the angel of the Church will suffer much persecution; hence Jesus comforts him concerning Him experiencing being first and also being last; Jesus also comforts him concerning resurrection

[41] Defined as "myrrh" in Matthew 2:11 and John 19:39; which is related to the suffering of death.

[42] This statement may have been said as a comfort to this Church which was encouraged to remaining faithful even to death; because there is the surety of resurrection through Jesus Christ.

[43] It is "necessary" (binding) that we enter the kingdom through "much tribulation" (Acts 14:22); and it's by tribulation we are "counted worthy of the kingdom of God" (2 Thessalonians 1:4-5).

[44] The true Jew is described by Paul in Romans 2:28-29, as a person who is circumcised in the heart in the spirit. The true Jews are the children of the promise, not the natural Jews according to the flesh (Romans 9:1-13). With that said, the statement may also be against those who claim to be Christians; however, they are not circumcised in the heart by the Spirit and therefore are not true Jews either.

[45] Synagogues point to manmade buildings that we call Churches today. A Church building does not constitute a Church. "Church" is people who believe that Jesus is the Christ, the Son of the living God. Buildings are sheep sheds.

[46] Experiencing emotional changes is also considered suffering.

be you **believing** to death,[47] and I will give you a crown of life.

11 He that has an ear let him hear[48] what the Spirit says[49] to the churches; **the one-conquering** shall not be hurt of the second death.[50]

12 And to the angel[51]of the church in Pergamos[52] write these things say he which has the sharp sword with two-edges.

13 I know your works, and where you dwell, where Satan's **throne**[53] and you hold fast my name, and have not denied my

---

[47] Compare Revelation 12:11.

[48] Faith comes by hearing preachers (Romans 10:14); hearing comes through the Word (declarations) of God (Romans 10:17); Faith also comes by God waking our ears to hear morning by morning (Isaiah 50:4-5). Sometimes our ears must be opened (lit., dug) in order for us to hear (Psalms 40:6). The more we "prick the ear" to hear, the more Jesus gives to us (Mark 4:23-25).

[49] The Spirit of God speaks "explicitly" as defined in First Timothy 4:1.

[50] Two types of death: death when a person leaves the earth until the resurrection and the second death (the lake of fire and brimstone). The second death having no authority over them is also said of those who will participate in the first resurrection (Revelation 20:6).

[51] Jesus' specific introduction of certain traits of His to each angel of the Church usually shows His calling and/or purpose for the angel and Church. In this case, Jesus manifests Himself as the sharp two-edged sword to fight against "them" in this Church that held the practice of Balaam and the conquest of laity.

[52] Literally: Much (per)-marriage ("gamos"); symbolic of churches that marry everything and anything. This was a city full of idolatry that married every so called "movement."

[53] Pergamos (located in modern day Turkey) became the throne of Satan, maybe through the murderous idolatrous practices of that time, i.e. man worship, demon worship, etc. Satan gave his throne to the beast in Revelation 13; hence the beast is a Satan worshipper.

faith, even in those days wherein Antipas[54] my **believing** martyr, who was slain among you, where Satan dwells.

 14 But I have a few things against you, because you have them there that hold the doctrine[55] of Balaam,[56] who taught Balak[57] to cast a stumbling block before the children of Israel, to eat things sacrificed to idols, and to **prostitute**.[58]

15 So have you also them that hold the doctrine of the Nicolaitans,[59] which thing I hate.

---

[54] Transliterated: Anti-everything ("pas")—his name points to why he was martyred (he was against all the idolatry and sins of Pergamos).

[55] There is the doctrine of Balaam (Revelation 2:14); he taught Balak how to cause Israel to commit a sin (anal sex mixed with idolatry) that would cause a death plague (Number 31:16 w/Numbers 24). There is the error of Balaam, he presumptuously "went" without being "called" because of money (Numbers 22:20-21 w/Jude 1:11). There is the way of Balaam, the love of payment of unrighteousness (2 Peter 2:15)

[56] Hebrew defined as: not of the people, or failure of the people

[57] Hebrew defined as: waster, annihilator

[58] This is in reference to "whoredom" of Numbers 25. The Hebrew word for "commit whoredom" in Numbers 25:1 is translated as "ekporneuo" in the Septuagint (LXX). "Ekporneuo" is defined as intensified fornication and is associated with homosexuality and sex with strange flesh (angels with women, men with demons, men in men, women with women) as revealed in the book of Jude. This intense fornication in Numbers 25 becomes apparent if one studies the rest of Numbers 25 with regards to Cozbi (the lie) and Zimri (musical) and their apparent public practice of anal sex (sex with the strange flesh). In n Numbers 25:8, the Hebrew words for "the tent" (הקבה) and "belly" (קבתה) is related to the Hebrew words for "curse" (Numbers 23:8) and "anus" by root according to Gesenius dictionary. The Hebrew word picture for this root (קבה) is "what comes from (ה) the house's (ב) rear (ק)." Cozbi (the lie) also points to same sexuality according to Romans 1:23-27.

[59] Conquer-laity; and this can relate to lording over God's flock (1 Peter 5:1-3).

16 **Change-mind**; or else **I-am-coming** to you **swiftly** and will fight against them with the sword of my mouth.[60]

17 He that has an ear, let him hear what the Spirit says to the churches; **to-the one-conquering** will I give to eat of the hidden manna, and will give him a white stone,[61] and in the stone a new name[62] written, which no man knows except he who receives.

18 And to the angel[63] of the church in Thyatira[64] write; these things say the Son of God, who has his eyes like to a flame of fire,[65] and his feet like **copper-incense**.[66]

19 I know your **acts**, and love, and service, and faith, and your **endurance**, and your **acts**; and the last more than the first.

---

[60] Symbolic of God's Word (logos (spoken/written sentence with rhema and name) and/or rhema (declarations from living person)) of God—Hebrew 4:12, Eph. 6:17.

[61] A stone used for voting on behalf of. Jesus votes for us.

[62] As Jesus gave Peter, John, James, etc. new names that summarized their personalities, and as the angel renamed Jacob, Israel, so likewise Jesus will rename the messenger(s) of this type of Church if they overcome.

[63] The angel of this Church is supposed to walk in the ability of Jesus' discerning eyes that can see the hearts (intents of the hearts) and the spiritual kidneys (related to the end of a thing (Jeremiah 12:2)); and this angel is also supposed to walk in prayer (incense) and judgment (copper). Paul's ministry reached some in this area (Acts 16:9-15).

[64] Defined by some as "affliction"

[65] God's "look" can be felt physically—in Exodus 14:24-25, God's look caused the wheels of Pharaoh's chariots to fall off. See also Psalms 11:4 4/11:6, Proverbs 20:8; Isaiah 30:10 ("prophesy" is defined as "gaze")

[66] Incense is symbolic of "prayer" (Revelation 5:8, Psalms 141:2); "prayer" in Psalms 141:2 is defined as intercession, to judge, etc. Hence Jesus manifesting to this Church as "feet with copper-incense" points to His judgment through His intercession against those sinning in this Church.

20 Notwithstanding I **have against you,**[67] **that** you **tolerate your wife**[68] **Jezebel,**[69] which calls herself a prophetess, and teach and **cause-to-stray** my servants to **prostitution** and to eat **image-sacrifices.**

21 And I gave her time[70] **to change-her-mind; and she does not want change-her-mind of her prostitution.**

22 Behold, I will cast her into a bed, and them that commit adultery with her into **mega** tribulation,[71] except they **change-mind out-of** their **acts.**

23 And I will kill her children with death;[72] and all the churches shall know that I am he who searches the **kidneys**[73] and hearts; and I will give to every one of you according to your **acts.**

24 But to you I say, and to the rest in Thyatira, as many as have not this doctrine,[74] and which have not known the

---

[67] This was directed to the angel (messenger(s)) of this Church as His custom is. Hence, the messengers of the Church are responsible for the actions within a ministry.

[68] The angel of this Church was married to Jezebel; and therefore, the angel is a man, as the angels with the seven bowls of wrath are men (Revelation 22:8-9).

[69] Named after the witch and wife of Ahab; Jezebel is defined as "Baal exalts," "Baal is husband to," or chaste ("un-husband"); her name may point to her lesbianism in secret, in addition to her public prostitutions.

[70] The mercy of Jesus always gives time to repent (change (your) mind).

[71] Great tribulation is defined in Matthew 24, Acts 7, Revelation 7, etc.

[72] One of the few times that Jesus judges a person with the penalty of death for the children.

[73] The Hebrew word for kidney means "something prepared" and is from a root word that is defined as "end;" hence Jesus' eyes of flames of fire has the ability to see the "end" results of people's action.

[74] According to Acts 16, Paul was instrumental in saving some who were form Thyatira (Lydia); perhaps this may the reason why some refused share in the doctrine of Jezebel.

depths[75] of Satan,[76] as they speak; I will put upon you none other burden.

25 But that which you have, **you-hold** until I **arrive**.[77]

26 And **the one-conquering**, and keeps my **acts** to the **finish**, to him will I give **authority** over the nations.[78]

27 And he shall **shepherd** them with a rod of iron;[79] as the vessels of a potter shall they be **together-crushed**; even as I received of my Father.

---

[75] Hosea 9:9 discussed the "deep corruption" of Israel as in the days of "Gibeah" which points to homosexuality and gang rapes as documented in Judges 19:16-26.

[76] What are the "depths of Satan" as it relates to Jezebel? Jezebel served Baal and she was a "Baal" worshipper (1 Kings 16:31). Jesus named "Baal" as "Satan" in Matthew 12. Hence the depth of Satan points to the practices of the Baal worship of Jezebel in the days of Elijah in addition to the practices Jezebel taught in the Church of Thyatira. Jezebel created false witnesses against people. She killed "Naboth" (fruit) to steal his vineyard and land (in other words Jezebel kills the fruit of God in people). She threatened and killed God's true prophets. She practiced witchcraft (whisperings and whispering of spells (strong impressions on the mind that mislead). She was a lesbian as revealed in her name. She was a prostitute and an adulteress.

[77] As indicated in Hebrews 10:37 "… the coming one, will arrive and will not delay."

[78] It appears to me that this is to be fulfilled during the millennium about to come.

[79] This phrase foremost was used for Jesus in Revelation 19:15. However, most of what applies to Jesus, the pattern Son, also applies to God's many sons (Revelation 12:5; 2:23); and according to Psalms 2:7-9, Revelation 2:23 is a sonship principle. David gathered the courage to declare what God said of him and the Messiah, "I will declare the decree: the LORD has said unto me, you are my Son; this day have I begotten you. 8Ask of me, and I shall give you the heathen for your inheritance, and the uttermost parts of the earth for your possession. 9You shall break them with a rod of iron; you shall break them in pieces like a potter's vessel."

28 And I will give him the morning star.[80]

29 He that has an ear[81] let him hear[82] what the Spirit says[83] to the churches.

CHAPTER 3

1 And to the angel[84] of the church in Sardis[85] write these things says he that has the seven Spirits of God, and the seven stars; I know your acts, that you have a name that you live and are dead.[86]

2 Be watchful, and **stand-fast** the things which remain, that are **intending** to die; for I have not found your **acts filled** before **my** God.

3 Remember therefore how[87] you have received and heard, and **guard**, and **change-mind**. If therefore you shall not watch, I **shall-arrive** on you as a thief, and you shall not know what hour I will **arrive** upon you.

---

[80] The morning star is Jesus (Revelation 22:16); therefore, Jesus will give the conquerors in this Church the brightness of the Jesus.

[81] We are called to prick the ear to hear God (Jeremiah 23:18).

[82] Faith comes by hearing preachers (Romans 10:14); hearing comes through the Word (declarations) of God (Romans 10:17); Faith also comes by God waking our ears to hear morning by morning (Isaiah 50:4-5). Sometimes our ears must be opened (lit., dug) in order for us to hear (Psalms 40:6). The more we "prick the ear" to hear, the more Jesus gives to us (Mark 4:23-25).

[83] The Spirit of God speaks "explicitly" (see 1 Timothy 4:1).

[84] The angel of the Church walks in the manifestation of the seven Spirits of God and also had a ministry to leaders (the seven stars) through a life of watching (prayer, etc.).

[85] "Red ones," related to red (flesh (Greek: "sarx"))

[86] The phrase of "living yet dead" is linked to a lack of prayer and watching (Revelation 3:2; 1 Timothy 5:5-6).

[87] How did this angel previously "received and heard" from God? The answer is that he was a "watcher" as indicated in Revelation 3:2 and 3:3b.

4 Nevertheless you have a few[88] names in Sardis which have not **soiled** their garments; and they shall walk with me in white for they are worthy.

5 The one-conquering, the same shall be clothed in white[89] **garment;** and I will not blot out his name out of the Book of Life,[90] but I will confess his name before my Father, and before his angels.

6 He that has an ear let him hear what the Spirit says to the churches.

7 And to the angel[91] of the church in Philadelphia[92] write these things says he that is holy, he that is true, he that has the **locker** of David, he that opens,[93] and no man **locks;** except he that opens, and no man[94] shall open.

8 I **perceived** your **acts; be-perceiving,** I have set before you an open door,[95] and no man can **lock** it; for you have a little

---

[88] God will save the "few" as he did in the days of Noah, in which "few, that is, eight souls were saved" (1 Peter 3:20).

[89] Around 1992, the Lord said to me one night as I was in prayer, "be white (pure) and fear no man."

[90] This phrase by Jesus makes it clear that a name can be blotted out of the Book of Life if a person does not overcome "the name that you live and are dead." We overcome by watching and prayer through faith.

[91] The ministry of the messenger was that of holiness, truth, and the blessings of the open door as David possessed.

[92] Fond of brothers

[93] The Lord "opened" for David for conquest in war (2 Samuel 8:6, "preserve" is literally "to be open"). Jesus also opens for us to conquer in spiritual warfare.

[94] There are some doors of opportunity that only God can open; and once he opens a door for you no man can lock you out. Saying it another way, when it's your season for God to use you to His glory, no man can stop it. Remember Joseph!

[95] Is this the "open door" to heaven that John experienced? (Revelation 4:1-2)

strength, and have **guard** my Word, and have not denied my name.

9 Behold, I will make them of the synagogue of Satan, which say they are Jews, and are not,[96] but **are-falsifying;** behold, I will make them **arrive** and worship before your feet, and to know that I have loved you.[97]

10 Because you have **guarded** the Word of my **endurance**, I also will **guard** you **out-of** the hour of temptation, which **intending is-coming** upon all the **occupied-houses,** to try them that dwell upon the earth.

11 **Be-perceiving,** I come **swiftly;** hold that fast which you have, that no man takes your crown.

12 **The one-conquering** will I make a pillar[98] in the temple of my God, and he shall go no more out; and I will write[99] upon him the name of my God, and the name of the city of

---

[96] The true Jew is described by Paul in Romans 2:28-29 and Romans 9:1-13. With that said, the statement may also be against those who claim to be Christians (true Jews); however, they are not circumcised in their hearts by the Spirit; and therefore, are not true Jews. They only occupy a building (synagogue) that makes them appear to be the true Jews of the Church of Jesus Christ.

[97] Compare Malachi 1:2a; Romans 9:13a; Daniel 9:23. The Lord still speaks encouragement of His love towards us today.

[98] The Greek word for "pillar" is transliterated as "style." A study of "style" in Roman history is very interesting. Apostles are also called "pillars" in Galatians 2. Also reference 1 Kings 7:21 where the twin pillars (Jachin and Boaz) are discussed. These pillars represent Jesus and His corporate twin brother (he who overcomes).

[99] Written with the ink of the Holy Spirit 2 Corinthians 3:3

my God, new Jerusalem, which **is-descending** out of heaven[100] from my God; and my new name.[101]

13 He that has an ear let him hear what the Spirit says[102] to the churches.

14 And to the angel[103] of the church of the Laodiceans[104] write; these things say the Amen, the **Believing** and True Witness, the Beginning of the creation of God.

15 I know your works, that you are neither cold nor hot; **you-owe** to be cold or hot.

16 So then because you are warm and neither cold nor hot, **I-am-intending to-vomit** you out of my mouth.

---

[100] Jesus also "descended" from Heaven according to John 3:13. Therefore, the descent of New Jerusalem has an element of descent similar to Jesus. That is, Jesus descended from heaven by birth.

[101] Jesus also received a new name after His submission to die for us; "a name which is above every name; that at the name of Jesus every knee should bow of things in heaven and things in earth and things under the earth … (Philippians 2:8-11).

[102] The Spirit of God speaks "explicitly" (see 1 Timothy 4:1).

[103] The angel of this Church had a ministry of the gift of Amen (so be it), gift of believing (strong faith), true witnesses and a good understanding concerning the new creation man (Jesus and His Church). However, they allowed riches to usurp their calling.

[104] This is defined as "righteous-people," or "just-people." Is this the prosperity Churches of our day as demonstrated in verse 17?

17 Because you say, I am rich, and increased with goods, and have need of nothing;[105] and **perceive** not that you are **talent-tested**,[106] and **mercy-able**, and **beggar**, and blind, and naked.

18 I counsel you to buy of me gold tried in the fire,[107] that you may be rich;[108] and white **garment**,[109] that you may be clothed, and the **disfigure** of your nakedness do not appear;[110] and **in-anoint** eyes with **plaster,** that you may see.[111]

19 As many as I love, I **expose** and **discipline**;[112] be zealous therefore, and **change-mind**.

20 Behold, I stand at the door, and knock; if any man hears my voice, and opens the door, I will come in to him, and will **dine** with him, and he with me.

---

[105] Compare Hosea 12:7-8, "He is a merchant, the balances of deceit are in his hand: he loves to oppress. And Ephraim said, yet I am become rich, I have found me out substance; in all my labors they shall find no iniquity in me that was sin." This also sounds like the prosperity teaching that believes suffering is no longer acceptable. However, the Bible said that it is "binding" (necessary) that through much tribulation we enter the kingdom of God (Acts 14:22).

[106] Or, balance-tested, weight-tested, money (talent)-tested; or money-calloused

[107] Is this "gold tried in the fire" alluding to true faith in/of God instead of trusting in gold that perishes (1 Peter 1:7)?

[108] True riches are: riches of His goodness (Romans 2:4), riches of His glory (Romans 9:23, Ephesians 3:16), riches of the glory of His inheritance (Ephesians 1:18), riches both of wisdom and understanding (Romans 11:33), riches of His grace (Ephesians 2:7), riches of the full assurance of understanding (Colossians 2:2), and rich in mercy (Ephesians 2:4).

[109] White garments are washed with the red blood of the Lamb of God (Revelation 7:14).

[110] Compare Revelation 16:15 and its associated notes.

[111] Compare Jesus' statement in John 9:39-41.

[112] God disciplines those whom he "receives" (Hebrews 12:6).

21 The one-conquering[113] will I grant to sit with me[114] in my throne,[115] even as I also overcame, and am set down with my Father in his throne![116]

22 He that has an ear let him hear[117] what the Spirit says[118] to the churches.

CHAPTER 4

1 After this I **perceived**, and behold, a door opened in heaven; and the first voice which I heard as it were of a trumpet talking with me; which said, **walk-up here,** and I will show you things which must be hereafter.

2 And immediately I was in **to-with-Spirit**[119] and **perceived** a throne was **laid** in heaven, and **him-sitting** on the throne.

---

[113] Or "win" by defeating ones enemies

[114] This phrase "with Him" is also used in Revelation 20:4; 6 and appears to have the same implication. Studying the Tabernacle built by Moses, we can understand that reigning with Him, may mean reigning with Him right here on earth, as it also implies that we will reign with Him in heaven.

[115] Jesus sits in His throne as the High Priest (Hebrews 8:1).

[116] Jesus is in the Throne <u>with</u> His Father; therefore, in the first resurrection, part of our priestly duty is us being part of "the Throne of the 'great-togetherness'" as we are "with Christ" (Hebrews 8:1; Revelation 20:4-6).

[117] Faith comes by hearing preachers (Romans 10:14); hearing comes through the Word (declarations) of God (Romans 10:17); Faith also comes by God waking our ears to hear morning by morning (Isaiah 50:4-5). Sometimes our ears must be opened (lit., dug) in order for us to hear (Psalms 40:6). The more we "prick the ear" to hear, the more Jesus gives to us (Mark 4:23-25).

[118] The Spirit of God speaks "explicitly" (see 1 Timothy 4:1).

[119] Heaven is in the Spirit; it is not 4 million miles away. John became in the Spirit "immediately" after the invitation to ascend to heaven through the open door.

3 And he that **is-sitting** was to look upon like jasper and a sardine stone; and a rainbow[120] round about the throne, like **seeing** an emerald.

4 And round about the throne twenty-four **thrones;** and upon the **thrones** I saw twenty-four elders sitting, clothed in white garment; and they had on their **heads** crowns of gold.

5 And out of the throne **is-proceeding** lightnings and thunders and voices; and seven Lamps of fire[121] burning **before the thrones**[122] which are the seven Spirits of God.

6 And before the throne a sea of glass like **ice-frost** and in the middle of the throne, and round about the throne, four **living-things**[123] full of eyes before and behind.[124]

7 And the first **living-thing** like a lion,[125] and the second **living-thing** like a calf,[126] and the third **living-thing** had a

---

[120] Rainbow is also a symbol of God's glory (Ezekiel 1:28); symbol of His covenant with Noah not to destroy the earth by water, again (Genesis 9:13-15).

[121] The seven Spirits of God (see note for Revelation 1:4) is also known as the seven Lamps of fire which can relate to the light of salvation (Isaiah 62:1).

[122] The seven Lamps representing the seven Spirits of God are before the throne and the seven Spirits of God are also represented as the seven lamps on the seven candlesticks (lampstands); thus, for the Churches to be enlightened with light from the seven Lampstand they must also go before the Throne of God where the seven Spirits of God also dwells.

[123] These living things are seraphs not cherubs because they have six wings with one head each like the seraphs in Isaiah 6, as opposed to the cherubs in Ezekiel 1 that has four wings and four faces each

[124] The ability to see "all" is in the believers according to 1 John 2:20.

[125] Jesus manifested as King in the book of Matthew.

[126] Jesus is revealed as the servant (ox) in the book of Mark.

face as a man,[127] and the fourth **living-thing** like a flying eagle.[128]

8 And the four **living-things** each of them, had six wings **around;** and full of eyes within; and they **up-pause** not day and night, saying,[129] **holy, holy, holy Lord God Almighty,** who was, and is, and is to come.

9 And **whenever** those **living-things** give glory and honor and thanks **to-the one-sitting** on the throne, **to-the one-**living **into the ages of the ages.**

10 The twenty-four[130] elders **sitting** on the throne fall down before him, and worship him[131] that lives **into the ages of the ages,** and cast their crowns before the throne, saying:

11 You are worthy, **our Lord and God,** to receive glory and honor and power; for you have created all things, and **through** your **will**[132] they **existed** and were created.

---

[127] Jesus is revealed as the perfect man in the book of Luke.

[128] Jesus is revealed as the ascended one in the book of John.

[129] Nominative case; therefore, they also personified worship.

[130] Twenty-four is the number that represents priesthood (1 Chronicles 24); hence the 24 elders represent the priesthood of elders (senior leaders) that rule with Christ

[131] An example of worship that all preachers (elders) should follow while in Church meetings, and not carry themselves like they are above worship by lingering in their offices doing nothing before they speak.

[132] The Greek word "thelema" can also be translated as "pleasure-will" or "glad-will;" we were created through pleasure.

CHAPTER 5

1 And I saw in the **right** of **him-sitting** on the throne a book written inside and on the back, sealed with seven seals.[133]

2 And I saw a **forceful** angel proclaiming with a mega voice, who is worthy to open the book, and to loose the seals thereof?

3 And no man in heaven, or in earth, neither under the earth, was able to open the book, neither to look **at-same.**

4 And I wept much, because no man was found worthy to open and to read the book, neither to look **at-same.**

5 And one of the elders says to me, weep not, **be-perceiving,** the Lion of the tribe of Judah, the Root of David, has **conquered** to open the book, and the seven seals thereof.

6 And I perceived and perceiving in the middle of the throne[134] and of the four **living-things,** and in the middle of

---

[133] The Spirit is the "seal" (Ephesians 1:13); and there are the seven Spirits of God (Revelation 4:5; 5:6) that coincide with the seven seals that the Lamb of God loosed.

[134] In the great ivory throne built by Solomon was a "footstool" in 2 Chronicles 2:18. The Hebrew word for "footstool" in 2 Chronicles 2:18 is also translated as "lamb" in Leviticus 9:3 and Ezekiel 46:13. It was also six (6) paces (a journey to a higher place) to the footstool (the lamb). Therefore, it can be 6,000 years of paces counting from the first Adam to the judgment seat (Greek: bema (footstool) of Christ mentioned in 2 Corinthians 5:10 and Romans 14:10. Note: According to 2 Corinthians 5:10, appearing before the footstool of Christ is a past and present reality (aoristic tense); however in Romans 14:10, it is "future" in tense which can point to the future coming of Jesus to judge before the millennium rule (1 Corinthians 4:3-5).

the elders, stood a Lamb[135] as having-been-slain,[136] having seven horns and seven eyes, which are the seven Spirits of God sent forth into all the earth.

7 And he came and took the book out of the right of him **sitting** upon the throne.

8 And when he had taken the book, the four **living-things** and twenty-four elders fell down before the Lamb, having every one of them harps, and golden **bowls** full of **incense**, which are the prayers of saints.

9 And they **are-singing** a new song, saying, you are worthy to take the book, and to open the seals thereof; for you were slain, and have redeemed to God **in** your blood **out-of** every kindred, and tongue, and people, and nation;

10 And have made **them** to our God **a kingdom**[137] and priests;[138] and **they** shall reign on the earth.[139]

---

135 Jesus, the Lamb of God that takes away our sin (John 1:29; 1:35). Note: he walks like the Lamb in public (John 1:29; Revelation 5:5); however, He functions as the Lion of the tribe of 'Praise' (Judah) in conquest (Revelation 5:5).

136 Jesus still has the nail prints (John 20:25-29); he is still a freshly slain sacrifice (in Hebrews 10:20 "new" is defined as "recently (freshly) slain.")

137 This same phrase ("a kingdom and priests") is used in Revelation 1:6 in reference to "us" who belong to Jesus.

138 One of the functions of being a priest of God during the millennium is the "ministering" (lit., priest-work) of the gospel of God (see Romans 15:16). The Church must remember that she is a royal priesthood of Jesus' Melchizedek order; and if that is understood, the book of Revelation is filled with the function of Jesus our Great-High Priest and His priests administering the priesthood, seen in pictures or signs like "the temple of God" the golden altar, the seven lampstands, priests in their linen garments with the belts, the Ark of the Covenant, God's Throne, the Mercyseat, and so on.

139 This can be understood in the function of the tabernacle of Moses. All the furniture, including the Ark (the Throne of Grace) was placed on the earth; hence

11 And I beheld, and I heard the voice of many angels round about the throne and the **living-things** and the elders; and the number of them was ten thousands times ten thousands, and thousands of thousands;[140]

12 Saying with a loud voice, worthy is the Lamb that was slain to receive power, and riches, and wisdom, and strength, and honor, and glory, and blessing.

13 And every creature[141] which is in heaven, and on the earth, and under the earth, and such as are in the sea, and all that are in them, I heard[142] saying, blessing, and honor, and glory, and power, to him that sits upon the throne, and to the Lamb **forever and ever. Amen.**

14 And the four **living-things** said, amen. And the elders fell down and worshipped.

---

we shall also reign on earth (compare/contrast Revelation 20:4-6; Revelation 3:21).

[140] 10,000 x 10,000 x 1,000s x 1,000s =100 Trillion at a minimum

[141] Including the "flood" (Psalms 98:8); including trees (Isaiah 55:12); see also Romans 8:35-39 where other created things as "tribulation," "distress," "famine," "height," "depth'" etc. are called "who" (hence personified).

[142] In the Spirit of the Lord, we have the ability to hear from all four realms. The same is true in the reverse, our preaching, and the declaration of the name of Jesus can be heard in all four dimensions (Philippians 2:9-11). For example, the trumpeting of the 7th Angel also involves judging the dead as Jesus' preaching judged the dead in hell, while he was there for 3 days (Revelation 11:18 w/1 Peter 3:19 and1 Peter 4:6).

CHAPTER 6

1 And I saw when the Lamb opened one[143] of the **seven** seals,[144] and I heard, as it were the noise of thunder,[145] one of the four **living-things**[146] saying, come and look.

2 And **I-perceived and be-perceiving** a white horse[147] and he[148] sitting on him had a bow; and a crown[149] was given to him; and he went forth conquering, and to conquer.

3 And when he had opened the second seal,[150] I heard the second **living-thing** say, come.

---

[143] Per Dr. Joshua (Turnel) Nelson of Trinidad, one of the ways the seals can be interpreted is looking at the seals in 360 year cycles; and after I researched his teaching, the years do seem to correspond with historical events. With that said, the opening of the seals is in the aoristic tense, which means the event happened in the past with ongoing actions and has no limit as to repetition (it has happened, it is happening, and it will happen again).

[144] The Spirit is the seal (Ephesians 1:13). Thus, this seal is the first of the seven seal of the Spirit; the seal of the Spirit of the Lord. This seal being opened demonstrates the lordship of Jesus by His conquest of the habitable world through His gospel of peace (the bow with no arrow).

[145] This voice of **thunder** can represents God glorifying His name again through the rider on the white horse (John 12: 27-31).

[146]God's seraph with their six wings participating in the opening of the first four seals.

[147] Is this the same white horse Jesus rode in Revelation 19:11? I believe so.

[148] Jesus conquered most of the world through the gospel for the first 360 years of Christianity (AD 30 through AD 390). AD 390, Christianity became the official religion of the Roman Empire. With that said, the Roman Catholicism has now corrupted the understanding of Jesus Church through the various idols of corruptible men and women and harlotry with unbelieving rulers of nations (Romans 1:23-27, Revelation 17, Revelation 18).

[149] Victor's crown glorifying God's name

[150] The era of wars from AD 390 to AD 750 (the second 360 years after Jesus' ascension) (and yes there are usually wars in every age). This second seal that was loosed is the seal of the Spirit of Wisdom. Maybe refusal of the wisdom of

4 And there went out another **horse of fire** and **it-was-given** to **him-sitting** on him to take peace from the earth, and that they should kill one another; and there was given to him a mega **battle-knife.**

5 And when he had opened the third seal,[151] I heard the third **living-thing** say, Come and **look.** And **I-perceived** and **be-perceiving** a black horse; and **he-sitting** on him had a **yoke** in his hand.

6 And I heard a voice in the middle of the four **living-thing** say, a measure of wheat[152] for a **denarius,** and three measures[153] of barley[154] for a **denarius;** and the oil and the wine[155] not **you-should-hurt.**

7 And when he had opened the fourth seal,[156] I heard the voice of the fourth **living-thing** say, come and **look.**

God can result in wars; because the Wisdom from above is first pure, peaceable, gentle, easy to be persuaded, full of mercy and good fruits, not prejudice and not hypocritical (James 3:17). But the wisdom of the earth is bitter, full of strife, electioneering, and so on.

[151] 750 to 1110 (~360 years of famine and lack, yet there was spiritual healing through the Good Samaritan ministry of the oil and the wine (Luke 10:34)). This seal is the third seal of the Spirit of Understanding. Understanding establishes a house (Proverbs 24:3).

[152] The "good seed" Matthew 13:37-37

[153] Point to the imbalance of the value for the "good seed" and the higher value for the barley (bread of God's Word, or the miraculous provision of bread—John 6:13)

[154] Used for bread and points to the supernatural provision for the Church (John 6:13) as Ruth was given seven measures of barley.

[155] Oil and wine is used for healing (Luke 10:34).

[156] 1110 to 1470, the season of the bubonic plague where Death and Hell killed ~25% of the population of the earth (this percentage is a guestimate) ; another principle is: whenever 25% of a population is affected by plague, Death and Hell may be responsible. The seal of the Spirit of Counsel; that is they may have refused His counsel (advise) of proper living before Hi,.

8 And **I-perceived** and **be-perceiving** a greenish[157] horse; and his name that **sitting** on him was Death,[158] and Hell[159] followed with him. And **authority** was given to them over the fourth part of the earth, to kill with sword, and with hunger, and with death, and **under** the **beasts** of the earth.

9 And when he had opened the fifth seal,[160] **I-perceived** under the **sacrifice-place**[161] the souls of them that were slain for the Word of God, and for the testimony which they held.

---

157 Chlorine, or lit "green" (Revelation 8:7; 9:4; Mark 6:39); Death rides that which appears to be green, a symbol of life.

158 It seems to me that one of the purposes of Death was to produce life (1 Corinthians 15:36). However, rather than producing life with regards to humans, the "firstborn of death" was "hunger" or the calamity of death-famine that "holds" humans in the "king of Terror" (Death) (Job 18:12-14). However, Jesus overcame death-hunger when Jesus faced hunger during Jesus' 40 days of fasting; and Jesus overcame death's "hold;" because "God has raised up" Jesus out of the dead, "having loosed the pains of Death, because it was **not possible** that He should be held under him [Death]." Jesus now "hold" the key of Death (Revelation 1:18).

159 Hell is a "she;" her soul can be enlarged; there is no limit as to how wide she can open her mouth as she receives those who descend into her (See Isaiah 5:14).

160 1470 to 1830, the season of the inquisition that killed many innocent believers (Lutherans) who believed contrary to the Catholic system were killed by the Catholic, then the killing of the Protestants by the Lutherans, then the killing of the Ana Baptists who believed contrary to the Protestants, etc. This principle can also be seen between the Pharisees and Jesus. When Jesus bought about change from Law to Grace, the Pharisees killed him and some of His followers. This seal is the seal of the Spirit of His Might. Jesus said the traditions of men can make some of the words of God ineffective (Mark 7:13), maybe it took the might of the Spirit to empower reformations; and it also took his might to strengthen the persecuted reformers (Ephesians 3:16)

161 The Altar of Incense under which their souls were praying to God to meet out recompense to those who kill the saints .

10 And they cried with a mega voice, saying, how long, **the Owner,**[162] holy and true, do you not judge and avenge our blood[163] on them that dwell on the earth?

11 And white robes were given to every one of them; and it was said to them, that they should **pause** yet for a **micro time,** until their fellow servants also and their brethren **are-intending** be killed[164] as they, should be fulfilled.

12 And **I-perceived** when he had opened the sixth seal,[165] and **be-perceiving** there was a **mega** earthquake; and the sun[166] became black[167] as sackcloth of hair, and **the whole** moon became as blood.[168]

---

[162] Owner as defined here is from the Greek word "despotes" (owner, possessor).

[163] God avenged them as noted in the third bowl of God's wrath (Rev 16:4-7)

[164] Christians have been martyred, are being martyred and shall be martyred

[165] 1830 to 2190, the season of the rise of many false denominations that claim to be of the Lord, Jehovah Witnesses, Mormonism, the rapture theory, Seventh Day Adventist (legalistic base denomination), etc. This seal is the seal of the Spirit of knowledge; they refused the knowledge of the finished work of Jesus and invented antichrist ideologies.

[166] The sun can represent spiritual patriarchs (1 Corinthians 4:15), the moon can represent matriarchs (Titus 2:2); the stars can represent the sons and daughters (Genesis 37:9-10).

[167] Patriarchs (leaders) in the Church that are dirty

[168] This may point to death by persecution or a spiritual eclipse, where the lesser light of man eclipses the greater light of Jesus. When Jesus was crucified there was solar eclipse where the sun was darkened by the eclipse of the moon in which darkness were allowed to rule for a brief moment during the death of Jesus.

13 And the stars[169] of heaven fell to the earth, even as a fig tree cast her **unripe** figs, when she is shaken of a **mega** wind.[170]

14 And the heaven departed as a scroll when it is **coiled**; and every mountain[171] and island[172] were moved out of their places.

15 And the kings of the earth, and the **mega great-men**, and the **rich-men**, and the **chief-of thousands**, and the **powerful-men**, and every **slave**, and every **free-man**, hid themselves in the dens and in the rocks of the mountains.

16 And said to the mountains and rocks, fall on us, and hide us from the face of **him-sitting** on the throne, and from the **grasping-anger** of the Lamb;

17 For the **mega** day of his **grasping-anger**[173] is come; and who shall be able to stand?

---

[169] These fallen stars are compared to unripe figs; therefore, they represent believers who do not mature due to a lack of sunlight because the sun was made "dirty;" and they were fallen due to mega wind of doctrines (Revelation 6:13 w/Ephesians 4:14).

[170] Can represent the numerous erroneous doctrines that were invented during the 1800s (Ephesians 4:14).

[171] This shaking of every mountain includes the mountain of Babylon (Jeremiah 51:25).

[172] Island can point to literal Islands or isolated people in the sea of humanity.

[173] The phrase "day of his wrath" is used three (3) times in the Bible. In Job 20:28-29, the phrase is used in conjunction with the wicked losing the increase of his house. In the book of Revelation, the day of his wrath is connected to the Sixth Seal and the wrath of the Lamb of God. In Psalms 110 it is used in relation to Melchizedek in the day the Lord will strike through kings.

CHAPTER 7

1 And after these things **I-perceived** four angels standing on the four corners of the earth, holding the four winds of the earth, that the wind[174] should not blow on the earth, nor on the sea, nor on any tree.

2 And I saw another angel ascending from **rising of-sun**, having[175] the seal[176] of the living God; and he cried with a **mega** voice to the four angels, to whom it was given to hurt the earth and the sea,

3 Saying, hurt not the earth, neither the sea, nor the trees, until we[177] have sealed[178] the servants of our God in their foreheads.[179]

---

[174] The wind of the 6th seal (Revelation 6:13); may also point to "wind of doctrines" (Ephesians 4:14)

[175] Literally, "holding the seal of God;" therefore, God's seal is linked to the laying on of hands (Acts 19:6 w/Acts 19:1-6)

[176] The Spirit is the seal (Ephesians 1:13, 4:30); and this seal is the seal of the Spirit of the Fear of the Lord. The Lord will be feared.

[177] This "one" angel called himself "we." Does this mean that the angel represents a corporate company of messengers? I think so!

[178] There are three sealing—circumcision of the heart by the Holy Spirit, baptism of the Holy Spirit, and the Holy Spirit of God writing on our foreheads (mind).

[179] Ezekiel 9:4-5 is an example of this people being sealed for protection. The Hebrew letters for mark, used in Ezekiel 9:6, is the pictographic symbol of a cross and a nail; and the word mark is also defined as "signature" (Strong's Concordance #8427).

4 And I heard the number of them which were sealed; a hundred forty-four thousand[180] sealed **out-of** all the tribes[181] of the children of Israel.

5 Out-of the tribe of Judah[182] sealed twelve thousand. **Out-of** the tribe of Reuben[183] sealed twelve thousand. **Out-of** the tribe of Gad[184] sealed twelve thousand.

6 Out-of the tribe of Asher[185] sealed twelve thousand. **Out-of** the tribe of Naphtali[186] sealed twelve thousand. **Out-of** the tribe of Manasseh[187] sealed twelve thousand.

---

[180] First, this applies to the first-fruit Jews that were saved from the days of John the Baptist until God turned from the Jews to the Gentiles in Acts 13:46. These Jews in those days were called "some" of Jesus' first-fruit (James 1:18, "a kind of firstfruits" (KJV), literally reads "some of the first-fruit...."). Second, these can also apply to the first-fruit true Jews (the Church according to Paul in Romans 2:28-29), the first-fruit of the Israel of God (Romans 9:6-9 w/Galatians 6:15-17).

[181] Dan (the judge) is not listed in the 12 tribes in this Chapter. Maybe his tribe (those whom God as deemed as judges) is the ones doing the sealing? Ephraim is also not listed; Joseph supplanted this tribe.

[182] Praise or worship now endowed to be "first." Jesus, of the tribe of praise, now has the "birthright" of the firstborn.

[183] Behold a son; and his name points to the Son Jesus who we behold when he saves us. This tribe that corresponds with its gate that points to the beginning of our salvation when we behold the Son, Jesus.

[184] Troop, army, overcome, attacker

[185] Happy, prosperous

[186] My wrestling, and points to God wrestling with us in order to change us.

[187] To forget my toils, a principle of forgiveness

7 Out-of the tribe of Simeon[188] sealed twelve thousand. **Out-of** the tribe of Levi[189] sealed twelve thousand. **Out-of** the tribe of Issachar[190] sealed twelve thousand.

8 Out-of the tribe of Zebulon[191] sealed twelve thousand. **Out-of** the tribe of Joseph[192] sealed twelve thousand. **Out-of** the tribe of Benjamin[193] sealed twelve thousand.

9 After this **I-perceived**, and, **be-perceiving** a **much** multitude, which no man could number, of all nations,[194] and kindred, and people, and tongues, **stood before the throne,[195] and before the Lamb**, clothed with white robes, and palms in their hands;

10 And cried with a mega voice, saying, salvation to our God which sits upon the throne, and to the Lamb.

11 And all the angels stood round about the throne, and the elders and the four **living-things**, and fell before the throne on their faces, and worshipped God,

---

[188] Hearer, the ability to hear the Spirit of Jesus

[189] Joined; one who is joined to Jesus and His Church.

[190] To pay the price; there is recompense; this tribe is known for understanding times and what Israel (the Church) ought to do; because they paid the price of suffering with Jesus.

[191] Habitation, dwell with me, exalted, he knows how to access the resources of the sea of humanity. We are to become a habitation of God through the Spirit.

[192] He (God) shall add another son; He (God) shall add (promotion, wealth, etc.)

[193] The son of power, the son of the right hand, the son of faith; we can't see our older brother Jesus (Joseph) until we bring Benjamin and walk out-of His right hand of power through faith.

[194] As is the pattern, the turn came for the gospel to be preached to the Gentiles after the first-fruit remnant of the Jews were sealed and saved (Revelation 7:9 w/Revelation 7:1-8; Revelation 14:6 w/Revelation 14:1-5).

[195] This multitude of believer without numbers were/are before the throne of God and the Lamb, therefore they are in the Holy of Holies, the temple of God.

12 Saying, amen! The blessing, and the glory, and the wisdom, and the thanksgiving, and the honor, and the power, and the **forcefulness** to our God into the ages of ages, amen!

13 And one of the elders answered, saying to me, what are these which are arrayed in white robes, and where came they?

14 And I said to him, **my Lord,**[196] you **perceived**. And he said to me, these are they which **are-coming**[197] out of **the mega** tribulation,[198] and have washed their robes, and made them white in the blood of the Lamb.

15 Therefore are they before the throne of God and serve him day and night in **his temple;**[199] and he **that-is-sitting** on the throne shall **tent** among them.

16 They shall hunger no more, neither thirst anymore; neither shall the sun[200] **fall** on them, nor any heat.

---

[196] Believer in Jesus Christ, who are sons of God, are also "lords" (Galatians 4:1-7; Galatians 3:26).

[197] "Are coming" is present tense in all the Greek texts; this means that the great tribulation happened in the days that John saw the vision.

[198] Great tribulation is also related to famine, or hunger—Acts 7:11, Revelation 7:14 w/7:16; the persecution of the Church in the days of John could also be called great tribulation as indicated in Revelation 7:14; the destruction of Jerusalem by Titus is also called great tribulation in Matthew 24:21. See also Acts 14:22 that discusses the "necessity" of "much tribulation," 1 Thessalonians 3:3-4 where Paul said we are "appointed" to tribulation, and 2 Thessalonians 1:4-5 where Paul said that tribulation makes us worthy and it is the righteous judgment of God. Hence, no one will escape and tribulation whether "great" or "much."

[199] This multitude of believer in the Lamb of God are "his temple;" therefore, they are also filled and sealed with the Holy Spirit (1 Cor 3:16, 1 Cor 6:19, 2 Cor 6:16, Eph 1:13).

[200] See Matthew 13:6 w/Matthew 13:21 where "sun" is symbolic of tribulation or persecution that arises because of the Word of God.

17 For the Lamb which is in the middle of the throne shall **shepherd** them and shall lead them **to fountains of waters of life;** and God shall wipe away all tears from their eyes.

CHAPTER 8

1 And when he had opened the seventh seal,[201] there was **hush** in heaven **as** half an hour.[202]

2 And I saw the seven angels which stood before God; and to them were given seven trumpets.[203]

---

[201] 2160 to 2520; however, since the seventh seal consists of the seven trumpets, and the day of trumpets occurs on the first day of the seventh month, it follows that at the end of this current 2,000 years is the beginning of the seventh millennium (the seventh month); therefore, some of the trumpets appear to overlap the sixth seal at the end of the current 2,000 years of the existence of the Church; and thus, the sounding of the trumpets can overlap up to "one day" past 2,000 up to 2,033 (one (1) prophetic day=1000 years/30 days=~33 years/day). This seal is the opening of the Spirit of the fear of the Lord. The Lord will expand the fear of the Lord in the earth through this seal and through all the judgments of the seven bowls of wrath.

[202] May be symbolic of ~21 years (1,000 years/24 hours=41.67 years/hour; hence a ½ of hour is ~42/2=~21 years; or it may be symbolic of one-half of a full prophetic week of years (360/24=15 years/hour; 15 years=1 hour; hence ½ hour=7.5 years or 7 years depending on the true Hebrew calendar year based on 7 days/week).

[203] "Given seven trumpets" can mean they were "gifted" to be prophets (Ezekiel 33).

3 And another angel[204] came and stood at the altar,[205] having **golden frankincense**;[206] and there was given to him much incense,[207] that he should **give to-the** prayers of all saints upon the golden **sacrifice-place**[208] which was **before the throne.**[209]

4 And the **smoke** of the incense **to-the** the prayers of the saints, ascended up before God out of the angel's hand.

---

[204] This angel represents Jesus our Gret-High Priest after the order of Melchizedek who minister at the Golden Altar of Incense (offering prayer of the saints to God and he always makes intercessor for us) as Aaron did on the day of Atonement (Leviticus 16, Hebrews 7, Hebrews 9, Romans 8). The angel also represents the priesthood of God's human messenger who minister before the living God, our Father and the Lamb of God mixing the prayers of the saints with the heavenly fire of the Altar through the fire ignited by the Holy Spirit (Mat 3:11, Acts 2:3-4).

[205] This is the Golden Altar of Incense also represents Jesus and the Holy Spirit our intercessors (Romans 8:26-27; Romans 8:34, Hebrews 7:24-28).

[206] The incense for the Altar of Incense had frankincense as one its ingredients, "pure frankincense," clean, white frankincense; however, in heaven the frankincense is golden (good opinion, good impression—gold can equal glory (good opinion, high estimation, etc.) Hebrews 9:5 w/Ex 25:18.

[207] Incense is symbolic of prayer (Revelation 5:8, Psalm 141:2).

[208] It appears to me that something similar to this event happened in the natural at the change of the Law age to the current age of Jesus' Grace. In Luke 1:8-17, we learn that Zachariah, the High Priest was before the Altar of Incense, a time of prayer, when Gabriel, an Archangel, introduced himself and indicated the changes that were about to be implemented through John, the Baptist, the son of Zachariah. Therefore, this similar event in Revelation 8:1-8 may also happen at the change from this age to the next millennium, the age of Jesus' mercy seat that has an end.

[209] The golden altar being "before the throne" shows that prayer and intercession is a Holy of Holies principles as seen that the "seven Spirts of God" is also "before the throne" and also declared so by Hebrews 9:4.

5 And the angel took the **frankincense**,[210] and filled it with fire[211] of the altar, and cast into the earth;[212] and there were voices,[213] and thunders,[214] and lightnings,[215] and an earthquake.[216]

---

[210] The word translated as "censer" in the King James Version is properly translated as frankincense which represents prayer, intercession. Or the censer has frankincense that is then fumigated with the fire of the altar ignited by the fire of the Holy Spirit (Mat 3:11, Acts 2:3-4).

[211] In Leviticus 16, the High Priest offered incense mixed with fire once a year on the 10th day of the 7th month. Jesus already fulfilled this feast of Atonement literally and in principle (Hebrews 9); just as Jesus fulfilled Passover, Jesus fulfilled sheaf of firstfruit resurrection from the dead, the Holy Spirit fulfilled the feast of Pentecost and so on. However, this date of the 7th month on the 10th day may also apply up to ~333 years into the 7th millennium (1,000 years/30 day=33.33 years/day x 10 days=333.33 years. However, please be reminded that all the feasts of the Old Testament is personified in Jesus and also to be personified in the Church without reference to time or duration.

[212] As the smoke from the fire mixed with the incense protected the High Priest from death in Leviticus 16:12-13, so this a protection for the priests of God in the earth before the judgments of the seven angels with the seven trumpets come to pass in order to protect the priesthood of believers during the trumpets.

[213] The power of God's clear sounding voices preparing his people for battles (1 Corinthians 14:7-11).

[214] God repeatedly indicating that he has glorified his name and will glorify it again (John 12:28-31).

[215] Lightning is from a Greek compound word "astrapto" which is literally translated as "star-fall" or "star-fly"(aster-star and pto-to fall or fly) also translated as "bright shining of a candle" (Luke 11:36); and thus, can represent stars of light causing one to see.

[216] Earthquake can be representative of God's signs of "shakings" caused by apostolic prayer and the company of the saints also praying with them in the "same-passion"(Acts 4:23-31).

6 And the seven angels[217] who had the seven trumpets[218] **internally-prepared**[219] themselves to **trumpet.**[220]

7 The first angel **trumpeted,**[221] and there followed hail and fire **mixed** with blood,[222] and they were cast upon the earth; **a third of the earth**[223] **was burned-down,** and the third of

---

[217] It appears that these seven angels have other as priest-prophets. It was seven priest who sounded the seven trumpets in Joshua 6, and these seven angels are in reference to God's temple where the golden ark is located also makes it clear that they are prophet priest.

[218] Prophets (watchmen) with prophetic ministry to predict, direct, judge and warn of impending events (Ezekiel 33; Jeremiah 6:17, 1 Corinthians 14:8-9)

[219] If, the ½ hour of silence prophetically points to ~21 years (1000 years/24 hours=41.6 years/hour), then it may take 21 years for these prophets to internally prepare themselves for the judgment they have to release. Moses was ready after 40 years on the backside of the desert, it is believed that Elisha washed the hands of Elijah for 20 years in preparation for the prophetic; Joshua waited 40 years to be assigned his ministry. If, the ½ hour points to 7.5 years [1 year for a day principle (360/24=15 years/hour; Numbers 14:34)], the principle of preparation as it relates to "years" still holds. Everyone is not necessarily like Paul and the 12 apostles that were prepared in approximately 3 ½ years. Jesus waited an additional 18 years to start His ministry at the age of 30 after the encounter at age 12 with the doctors in Luke 2:41-51.

[220] According to Leviticus 23, the Feast of Trumpets occurred on the first day of the 7th month; thus, these messengers can be sounding in the beginning of the 7th millennium for "one" day [~33 years (1,000 years/30 prophetic days=33.33 year per day)].

[221] What did this angel and the other angels trumpet (prophesy)? He (they) prophesied the very events that occurred, witnessing to their true calling to be prophets (trumpets). Note: the use of the word "trumpeted" for all the seven trumpets is in the aorist tense—a past action, with ongoing activity with no limit as to repetition (the trumpets have trumpeted, they are trumpeting and the shall trumpet). Aorist can be defined as "no boundary," or "no limit."

[222] It appears to me that throughout the book of Revelation blood is used as a judgment because humanity has rejected the most valuable blood of Jesus and has shed the blood of God's people.

[223] This will happen literally; yet it can be a symbol of a place where beasts come from (Revelation 13:11); or the place of bitterness, envy, strife, lies, evil work (James 3:14-16).

trees[224] was **burned-down**, and all green grass[225] was **burned-down**.

8 And the second angel **trumpeted**, and as it were a **mega** mountain burning[226] with fire was cast into the sea;[227] and the third of the sea became blood.[228]

9 And the third part of the creatures which were in the sea, **having soul,**[229] died and the third of the ships[230] were **through-rotted**.

10 And the third angel **trumpeted**, and there fell[231] a **mega** star[232] from heaven, burning as it were a lamp,[233] and it fell

---

[224] This will happen literally; yet it may point to the burning up of people ("trees") who trust more in "pedigree" rather than Jesus (Matthew 3:9-10 w/Hebrews 7:3).

[225] This will happen literally; yet it may have spiritual implication that God is going to burn up the flesh nature (sinful nature) of humanity and the glory of men. 1 Peter 1:24, indicates that "grass" is a symbol of "flesh" (carnal or sinful nature) and a symbol of the glory of man.

[226] According to Daniel 2:35 and Zechariah 4:7, the "great mountain" may be symbolic of the Church of Jesus and the Kingdom of God. This may also be a literal meteor that will fall from heaven into the sea causing a catastrophe.

[227] Literal sea or spiritually, the sea of humanity

[228] Fish breather water or oxygen, not blood; thus, death to creatures of the sea.

[229] Compare Matthew 16:24-25 ("life" is defined as "soul").

[230] Ships can symbolize ministries who do business on/with the sea of humanity

[231] This fall can be a result of the prediction (trumpet-prophecy) of the third angel. In other words, some will fall as a result of judgment executed by the prophets and apostles of God. Or this "star fall" causing bitterness is one of God's stars (messengers) deliberately permitted to fall to the earth to judge through bitterness that caused death

[232] This star can symbolize "bitter" messengers.

[233] Pretending to have the message of salvation (Isaiah 62:1)

upon the third of the rivers,[234] and upon the fountains[235] of waters.

11 And the name of the star is called **Absinth**;[236] and the third of the waters became **absinth**; and many men died of the waters,[237] because they were made **bitter.**

12 And the fourth angel **trumpeted**, and the third of the sun was **pounded**,[238] and the third of the moon, and the third of the stars; so as the third of them was **obscured**,[239] and the day not **may-be-lighten**[240] for a third of it, and the night **like-as.**

---

[234] Tongues that will be embittered by this bitter messenger

[235] According to James 3:10-11, "fountains" are the "mouths" of people that words (waters) flow from that are either bitter or sweet.

[236] Literally "undrinkable." There is a star called "Absinth" whose bitterness causes death.

[237] Men died from the water because they were not "sweetened" by the cross (tree) of Jesus (Exodus 15:23-26 w/1 Peter 2:24).

[238] In Jeremiah 23:33-40, some were "pounded" (in Jeremiah 23:33; 39 the word "forsake" in the KJV means "pound") who had perverted the word of the Lord and then called their perverted words the burden of the Lord.

[239] Some being "pounded" to "obscurity" may be a result of actions cited in Jeremiah 23:33-40. "Obscured" is also in the "active voice;" so they were the ones that would not give their light.

[240] An obscurity of the light of the gospel of Jesus due to the sun (patriarchs (fathers), the moons (matriarchs (mothers) and the stars (children) being pounded for perverting the words of God (Jeremiah 23:33-39—in Jeremiah 23:33; 39, "forsake" means "to pound")

13 And **I-perceived** and heard an **eagle**[241] flying **in** the **mid-heaven**, saying with a loud voice,[242] Woe, woe, woe, to the **dwellers** of the earth by reason of the **remaining** voices of the trumpet of the three angels, **of-is-intending to-be-trumpeting.**

CHAPTER 9

1 And the fifth angel **trumpeted**,[243] and **I-perceived** a star[244] fall[245] from heaven **into** the earth; and to him was given the **locker** of the **well of-the abyss**.

---

[241] This eagle may symbolize the corporate eagle ministry consisting of Jesus and His Church. One of the understandings of the Hebrew word picture for eagle [NShR—(N (נ) Sh (ש) R (ר)] can be the posterity or seed ((נ) of the Head or Prince (שר). Jesus is Head of the Church; and the corporate Body of Christ is the seed or posterity of Jesus Christ.

[242] Hosea 8:1 literally reads: "To the palate of you, **trumpet as eagle;**" therefore, this eagle (prophet) may have a ministry like the prophet Hosea; or allude to the harlot Babylon as Hosea dealt with Israel's harlotry.

[243] What did this angel and the other angels trumpet (prophesy)? He (they) prophesied the very event that occurred witnessing to their true calling as prophets (trumpets).

[244] Who is this star? He is not named as the star "wormwood" was named. He is not identified as the stars of the Churches were identified as angels (messengers) of the Churches; and these messengers of the Churches were men because at least one of them was married. Hence the question must be asked, "is this Jesus the "Star of Jacob" mentioned in Numbers 24:17, since the book is about the revelation of Jesus Christ? If this star is not Jesus, stars are supposed to lead people to Jesus (Matthew 2:1-10). Hence this star may be good, and the use of the word "fall" may be more descriptive rather than the star's nature. However, if none of the first two inferences are true, then this star maybe a fallen star (a former angel of the Church) that had the knowledge of God, which includes the ability to open the abyss.

[245] "Fall" is perfect tense in the Greek; hence this star fell before the trumpet sounded.

2 And he opened the **well of-the abyss;**[246] and there arose a smoke out of the pit, as the smoke of a **mega** furnace; and the sun[247] and the air[248] were **obscured** by reason of the smoke of the pit.

3 And there came out of the smoke locusts upon the earth; and to them was given **authority**, as the scorpions[249] of the earth have **authority**.

4 And it was commanded them that they should not hurt the grass of the earth, neither any green thing, neither any tree; but only those men which have not the seal[250] of God on their foreheads.[251]

5 And to them it was given that they should not kill them, but that they should be tormented **five months;**[252] and their torment as the torment of a scorpion, when he strikes a man.

---

[246] "By His (the Lord's) knowledge is the abyss 'cleaved open'" (Proverbs 3:20).

[247] Literal "sun" or spiritual patriarchs will be obscure, not being able to help during the fulfillment of this prophecy.

[248] These locusts from the abyss will even obscure the effects of the prince of the authority of the air due to the severity of the torment of this prophecy (Ephesians 2:1-2). Remember demons and/or fallen angels don't like to be sent to the abyss (Luke 8:31). This is proven out again in Revelation 20:1-3 when an angel had to use strength to bind Satan in order to cast him into the abyss. Angels must be afraid of King Abaddon or Apollyon, the angel of the abyss (Revelation 9:11).

[249] Greek: scatter-venom; Jesus gave believers authority over scorpions. (Luke 10:19).

[250] The Spirit is the seal (Ephesians 1:13); the seal in the forehead is the mind of Christ as a result of the Holy Spirit writing (2 Corinthians 3:3) on their foreheads (minds).

[251] A compound of two Greek words: "meta" (change, beyond, middle, with) and "ops" (eyes), to change the way one sees (eyes), or beyond the eyes (what is beyond forehead? the mind); forehead points to the way one sees and thinks; and therefore the seal of God in the forehead is the ability to see and think like Jesus.

[252] According to the Scriptures, five (5) months is a number that represents hiding (Luke 1:24 w/Revelation 9:5-6; Genesis 7:23-24).

6 And in those days shall men seek death and shall not find it; and shall desire to die, and death shall flee from them.

7 And the shapes of the locusts like to horses **internally-prepared** to battle; and on their heads as it were **crowns like gold,**[253] and their faces[254] as the faces of men.[255]

8 And they had **hair as the hair of women,**[256] and their teeth were as of lions.

9 And they had **chest**, as it were **chest** of iron;[257] and the sound of their wings as the sound[258] of chariots of many horses **running**[259] to battle.

10 And they had tails like to scorpions,[260] and there were stings in their tails; and their **authority** to hurt men five months.

---

[253] Crown of gold may indicate victors crown related to the kingdom (for gold crown is liken to "kingdom crown" in the book of Esther). These locust will be victorious in their judgments.

[254] The Greek word for "face" also means "appearance."

[255] Mankind will see the reflection of themselves in faces of these locust-scorpions.

[256] Hair as women may symbolize their submission to command of the king angel Abaddon (Compare Rev 9:4).

[257] Chests (breastplates) in the Scriptures are symbolic of love and faith (1 Thessalonians 5:8); symbolic of righteousness (Ephesians 6:14); therefore, these locust-scorpion will have iron love and iron faith. Or they will have unyielding righteous judgment against those who are not sealed.

[258] This type of sound causes fleeing (2 Kings 7:6-7).

[259] These horse like scorpions are fearless (Job 39:19-24).

[260] Scorpion can be defined as "scatter-venom" or "scatter-poison" (Interlinear Scripture Analyzer)

11 And they had a king[261] over them, the angel of the **abyss**, whose name in the Hebrew tongue, Abaddon,[262] but in the Greek tongue has a name, Apollyon.

12 One woe is past; **be-perceiving, are-come** two woes more **after these**.

13 And the sixth angel **trumpeted**,[263] and I heard a voice[264] from the four horns[265] of the golden **sacrifice-place**[266] which is before God,

14 Saying to the sixth angel which had the trumpet, loose the four angels which are bound in the **mega** river Euphrates.[267]

---

[261] Isaiah, Jeremiah, Daniel, the prophet, and the book of Job imply that there are numerous "king angels," or "king spirits," or spirit (invisible) princes.

[262] According to the book of Job 31:1-12; men who "plan" to commit adultery usually results in an encounter with fire that relate to the king angel, Abaddon.

[263] What did this angel and the other angels trumpet (prophesy)? He (they) prophesied the very event that occurred witnessing to their true calling as prophets (trumpets).

[264] Please refer to "Section #3 under the subtitle, "A Revelation from Jesus—the Sixth Trumpet."

[265] In Leviticus 16:18-19, the blood of the sacrifice was placed on the horns of the altar of incense once a year; Jesus fulfills this also with His blood sprinkling the things in heaven (Hebrews 9:21-23), Jesus' blood also speaks (Hebrews 12:24); hence the voice from the horn of the altar can be the voice of Jesus' blood directing this judgment

[266] The fact that the altar of incense is referenced may hint to a time just at the end of the Church age of 2,000 years.

[267] "Euphrates" is defined as: to break forth, to gush forth, or to rush forth, fruitfulness; the angels shall break forth and gush forth and multiply into 100,000,000 horsemen, at a minimum.

15 And the four angels were loosed,[268] which were **internally-prepared**[269] for an hour, and a day, and a month,[270] and a year, for to slay the third of men.[271]

16 And the number of the army of the horsemen **ten-thousands of-ten-thousands**,[272] and I heard the number of them.

17 And **in-this-way I-perceived** the horses in the vision, and **them-sitting** on them, having **chest** of fire, and of **hyacinth**,[273] and **God-sulfur-lightning-like;** and the heads of the horses as the heads of lions; and out of their mouths issued fire and smoke and **God-sulfur-lightning**.

---

[268] "Loosed" means "to be reduced down to its constituent particles" (Strong's Concordance); meaning the four (4) angels were loosed to become 100,000,000 horsemen.

[269] These angels were **internally prepared** for the express purpose of killing; therefore, they had to be bound only to be released when voiced by the horns of the golden altar of incense

[270] These angels can be released for one hour, if God so wills, they can be released for only a day if God so chooses, they can be released for a month (compare Hosea 5:7 where "a month shall devour them ..."), or they can be released for a year according to God's will; see also Numbers 9:22 where God sometimes operates in time increments of "days," "a month" and "a year."

[271] Maybe these men refused Jesus' atonement through His blood (Exodus 30:10); hence the voice from the four horns of the Altar of Incense.

[272] Psalms 68:17 literally reads in the Hebrew: "The chariots of God are tens of thousands, thousands **'changes,'** of the Lord." In other words, some angels and/or spirits can change and multiply themselves (comparer Revelation 16:13). In this case the four multiplied into 100 million.

[273] Hyacinth is also known in Greek mythology as a plant that was grown out of the blood of a young man (Hyacinth) that the Greek god, Zeus, had a homosexual relationship with and accidently killed. With that said, is this chest of hyacinth symbolic of judgment against the sexual bloodshed that is caused by homosexuals?

18 By these three was the third of men killed, by the fire,[274] and by the smoke,[275] and by the **God-sulfur-lightning**,[276] which issued out of their mouths.

19 For **the authority of the horses** in their mouth, and in their tails; for their tails like to serpents, and had heads, and with them they do hurt.

20 And the rest of the men which were not killed by these plagues yet not **they-changed-mind** of the **acts** of their hands, that they should not worship devils, and idols[277] of gold, and silver, and brass, and stone, and of wood; which neither can see, nor hear, nor walk;[278]

21 Neither **they-repented out-of** their murders,[279] nor **out-of** their **drugs-potion**, nor **out-of** their **prostitution**, nor **out-of** their thefts.

---

[274] This may include the fire related to fever.

[275] This smoke is the dark purple-bluish color smoke that relates to the color of hyacinth flower and this "smoke" can cause death.

[276] Greek, "theion"— "a place struck by lightning" and gives off a smell.

[277] There is a demon behind every idol (1 Corinthians 10:19-22).

[278] In Revelation 13:15, the false prophet had the ability to cause an image to speak; however, it could not cause that image to see, hear or walk.

[279] "Murder" as mentioned here is not limited to individual murder that occurs in the earth. Murder must also be considered in the context of genocide, ethnic cleansing, abortion, assassinations, terrorism, etc. That is, even though mankind experiences the plagues caused by murder, some still refuse to repent (change their minds to stop the killing). No man is to shed the blood of another man (Genesis 9:4-6); yet there is forgiveness in repentance to the Lord. Remember Moses, David and Paul who repented.

CHAPTER 10

1 And **I-perceived** another **forcible** angel[280] come down from heaven, clothed with a cloud;[281] and a rainbow[282] upon his head, and his face as the sun,[283] and his feet as pillars of fire.[284]

2 And he had in his hand a **book** open; and he set his right foot upon the sea and left on the earth.

3 And cried with a loud voice, as a lion roars;[285] and when he had cried, seven thunders[286] uttered their voices.[287]

---

[280] I believe this is Jesus in "another form" as the angel of the Lord—Mark 16:12; Joshua 3:1-6

[281] The cloud may be a symbol of people (Hebrews 12:1). God also speaks of His beloved Son—Jesus—from the cloud (Matthew 17:5).

[282] The rainbow is a symbol of the covenant **not** to destroy the earth by water again (Genesis 9:13-15). The rainbow is also symbol of God's glory (Ezekiel 1:28, Revelation 4:3).

[283] His face as the sun is one of the results of the Lord being transfigured into glory (Matthew 17:2). The sun is also a demonstration of the "power" of the Son (Revelation 1:16). That is, there is also the Sun of Righteousness (Jesus) with healing in His wings (Malachi 4:2).

[284] The pillars of fire are symbols of light the Lord uses to lead His people in the way by night (Exodus 13:21).

[285] This can be interpreted as the prophetic voice of God calling His sons from the sea (of humanity)—Hosea 11:10, where the word "west" is also translated as "sea;" Amos 3:8.

[286] The "God of Glory" thunders in seven thunders (Psalms 29:3); the "God of Glory" appeared/spoke to Abraham (Acts 7:2); the God of Glory is associated with the "seed" the Son and the seed of His many sons he will bring to glory (see Hebrews 2:10)

[287] This is related to the God of Glory calling for His "many sons" to be placed (adopted).

4 And when the seven thunders had **spoken** their voices,[288] **I-was intending** to write; and I heard a voice from heaven saying to me, seal up[289] those things which the seven thunders **spoke**, and write them not.

5 And the angel which I saw stand upon the sea and upon the earth lifted up his **right** hand to heaven.

6 And swore by him that lives forever and ever, who created heaven, and the things that therein are, and the earth, and the things that are **in her**, and the sea, and the things which are **in her**, that there should be time[290] no longer.

7 But in the days[291] of the voice of the seventh angel, **whenever he-is-intending trumpeting**, the **secret** of God[292]

---

[288] The Lord opened my understanding of this on August 1, 2008, from Psalms 29; Psalms 29:1, KJV reads "give unto the Lord O' you mighty;" and can be translated as "place unto the Lord sons of God." The purpose of the seven thunders appears to announce the placing of God's mature sons to glorify the Father as Jesus was placed as the Son to glorify the Father (see John 12:27-29).

[209] Apostles and prophets have the authority to seal or open mysteries if directed by the Lord Jesus.

[290] The Greek word "chronos" defined as "uninterrupted time." God is going to interrupt time with His sons, as Jesus interrupted time as outlined in Galatians 4. In other words, God's "sons [will be] "placed" (adopted) demonstrating the glory of the Father as Jesus was the placed Son of God demonstrating His glory. The interruption of uninterrupted time is to start in Revelation 12, when Zion birth her corporate children.

[291] This author believed the days of the 7th Trumpet is 1260 days, which includes, but not limited to, the work of the Two Witnesses in Revelation 11.

[292] This is the mystery as revealed by Jesus that God, our Creator, is to also be viewed as "our Father" and that Jesus is the Christ in us, the hope of glory (Colossians 2:2 w/Colossians 1:27).

was-finished,[293] as he has **evangelized**[294] to his servants the prophets.

8 And the voice which I heard from heaven spoke to me again, and said, go take the **booklet** which is open in the hand of the angel which stands upon the sea and upon the earth.

9 And I went to the angel, and said to him, give me the **booklet**. And he said to me, take and eat it up;[295] and it shall make your belly bitter,[296] but it shall be in your mouth sweet as honey.[297]

10 And I took the **book** out of the angel's hand and ate it up; and it was in my mouth sweet as honey; and as soon as I had eaten it, my belly was bitter.

---

[293] The mystery will be finished in twofold phases. It will be finished in the days of the voice of the seventh angel and whenever he is about to sound (which means that the mystery will also be finished in the days before he sounds).

[294] In 1 Peter 1:10-12, we learn that the Spirit of Christ that was in the prophets, testified of Jesus, His suffering, and the "glories" (us) who would come after Jesus as a result of Jesus giving His life for us.

[295] Ezekiel 2:9-3:4, like Ezekiel, John ate the very words he would speak (the words we are now reading in the book of Revelation from this verse forward).

[296] The actual dispensing of God's prophetic words or functioning in the prophetic ministry can be bitter at times (Ezekiel 3:14).

[297] God uses sweetness to start the process of accomplishing his will. If there was not pleasure in sex, would children be conceived? If there was not pleasure in eating (tasting and smelling), would we eat? Ministry may be bitter at times; yet God uses sweetness to bring a balance.

11 And **they** said to me, you must prophesy again[298] **upon** many people and nations, and tongues, and kings.[299]

CHAPTER 11

1 And there was given me a reed likened to a rod saying, rise and measure[300] the temple of God,[301] and the altar, and **them-worshiping in it.**

2 But the court[302] which is **outside**[303] the temple **you-cast-out** out and measure **her** not;[304] for it is given to the Gentiles; and the holy city[305] shall they tread under foot forty-two months.[306]

---

[298] Sometime the Lord asks prophets to "prophesy again." In other words, He may ask them to repeat prophesies (Ezekiel 47:4). As indicated previously, "prophesy again" may also mean that John would continue to prophesy again, with regards to what was written in the book that he ate (Ezekiel 2:9-3:4). In other words, after John digested the spiritual book, the words that were written in the book were in his spirit ready to be spoken.

[299] The people, nations, tongues, and kings point to John's international reach as spoken by the Lord Jesus.

[300] This is a measure for protection. In Ezekiel 41:3-4, the measure is a measure that defines. In Ephesians 4:13 w/4:16 the measure is for function.

[301] The Temple of God is the Body of Christ (1 Corinthians 3:16)

[302] "Yard" as open to the wind or air; hence open to every "wind of doctrine" and the wind of the prince of the authority of the air (Ephesians 2:2 and Ephesians 4:14).

[303] In Matthew 23:25-28, Jesus' definition of what it can mean to be more focused on "outside" is linked to a "hypocritical" lifestyle.

[304] Those who were NOT measured were unprotected would be trodden under foot. Thus, those are in the measure of the temple, altar and worshippers will be protected.

[305] May apply to the "cast outs" of New Jerusalem (Revelation 11:2 w/21:2; w/22:19)

[306] 42 is 6x7, and 6 is the number of man; 7 is the number of God's rest; therefore the 42 months is symbolic of mankind (666) against God (7)

3 And I will **give** to my two witnesses,[307] and **they shall prophesy**[308] a thousand two hundred **sixty** days,[309] clothed in sackcloth.

4 These are the two olive trees,[310] and the two candlesticks[311] standing before the **Lord** of the earth.

---

[307] The two witnesses are really four (2 candlesticks + 2 olive trees ≠ 2); so the "two witnesses" is true to "two" if you look at them represented by the two cherubs on the mercy-seat of the Ark; and yet the sum of the two witnesses (2+2=4) is also true represented by the four (4) cherubs in Solomon's Oracle, the two cherubs on the Ark, plus the other two cherubs of olive trees "carved for action" overshadowing the Ark with its mercy seat. The two witnesses are also twofold—the two olive threes (1) and the two candlesticks (2).

[308] The phrase ("and they shall prophesy") is used for those who prophesy by the Holy Spirit; and those who prophesy by the use of musical instruments in conjunction with the Holy Spirit (Acts 2:18, 1 Samuel 10:5, Numbers 11:25-26); contrast Jeremiah 23:21. There will be another outpouring of prophetic judgment through the Holy Spirit in conjunction with prophetic music and spontaneous songs of the Lord Jesus "in" and "through" His Church.

[309] This is the same time period as 42 months, except its written differently (1,260 days) to highlight (I believe) the different workings.

[310] Two olive trees made up of the Jews (cultivated olive tree) and Gentiles (wild olive tree)—see Romans 11:24; symbolized by the two cherubim of olive trees "carved for action" in the temple built by king Solomon; Zerubbabel (flow from Babylon) and Joshua (Salvation) in Zechariah seem to also be the historical reference to the two olive trees and points to the king-priest ministry of Jesus and His Church.

[311] The definition of the two witnesses is simple, they are the two(fold) candlesticks (churches); and they are the two olive trees (the Church made up of Jews and Gentiles); and the two(fold) olive trees are also called "sons of fresh (golden) oil (used to produce light)" in Zechariah 4.

5 And if any man will hurt them, **fire proceeds out of their mouth,**[312] and devours their enemies; and if any man will hurt them, he must in this manner[313] be killed.

6 These have **authority** to **lock** heaven that it rains not in the days **'of-the'** prophecy;[314] and have **authority** on waters to turn them to blood, and to smite the earth with all plagues, **as-many-times if-ever**.

7 And when they shall have finished[315] **the testimony,**[316] the beast[317] that **is ascending** out of **the abyss**[318] shall make war against them, and shall overcome them, and kill them.

---

[312] Fire proceeding out of their mouth is an idiom used of God's words (Jeremiah 5:14).

[313] The same method that people may mean to harm the two witnesses, the same method will be reciprocated to them as in Esther 9:2 w/Esther 7:10; and according to Daniel 2:44 and Daniel 7:14, God's kingdom cannot be destroyed ("lit., hurt, harm), unless of course God allows it after His purposes are completed as in Revelation 11:7 and as patterned by Jesus in the Gospels.

[314] "The prophecy" is "the testimony of Jesus" (Revelation 19:10, Revelation 1:3, Revelation 22:7; 10; 18; 19). In other words, not only is prophecy the ability to foretell; testifying of Jesus is also considered prophecy.

[315] They cannot be killed until God is finished with His plan—John 7:30; John 8:20; John 13:1.

[316] "The testimony" is Jesus via "the spirit of prophecy" (Revelation 19:10).

[317] The first mention of the beast; Revelation 12 and Revelation 13, at a minimum, take place before this. In fact, it appears that the 42 months, the 1260 days, the season, season, and half-a-season are all the same time period (Revelation 11:2; 11:3; Revelation 12:6; 12:14; Revelation 13:5).

[318] The dead (Romans 10:7), locusts (Revelation 9) also abided in the abyss

8 And their **fall** in the street of the **mega** city,[319] which spiritually is called Sodom[320] and Egypt, **wherever**[321] also **their** Lord was crucified.[322]

9 And they of the people and kindred and tongues and nations see their **fall** three days and a half and shall not **forgive** their **fall** to be put in graves.

10 And they that dwell upon the earth shall rejoice over them,[323] and make merry, and shall send gifts one to another;

---

[319] This is Mystery Babylon, **not** Jerusalem (see notes for Sodom and Egypt); in the oldest text and the Majority text this phrase ("great city") is only used of Mystery Babylon; in revelation 21:10, this phrase is excluded in all the Greek texts, except for one. It appears to me that Mystery Babylon are people who claim to have the "Bridegroom" (Jesus), yet commit spiritual fornication with idols, with ungodly leaders, relics, demons, etc.

[320] The state of the apostate primed for recruitment by the three beasts—Revelation 16. It must also be stated that legalization of same sex marriage does not make it acceptable to God (Leviticus 18:22; 20:13; Romans 1:26-27).

[321] Greek: "hostis" translated as "wherever" (compare its use in Luke 17:37). Translating "hostis" as "wherever" confirms the globalization of the "great city" as indicated in Revelation 17:15 w/17:18; and also shows that the martyrdom of the two witnesses is a global persecution against the Church of Jesus "wherever" Christ is symbolically being crucified again, by the killing Jesus' Church.

[322] "Crucified" is aoristic tense (the event occurred with no limit on repetition and duration)—the crucifixion happened, it is happening, and it shall happen until Jesus returns in His coming. With that said, "the great city" (the people of Mystery Babylon) that practices the practice of Sodom (Genesis 19) and the practices of Egypt (as exemplified by Jannes and Jambres in the power of occultism and enchantments (Exodus 7, etc.) is the same as these people crucifying Jesus again (compare Hebrews 6:6 w/Hebrews 6:1-5).

[323] Another proof that the two witnesses are the "first-fruit Christ" (the first to become like Jesus); that is, some rejoiced at Jesus' death (the first-fruit of the first-fruit), according John 16:20b, as the people of the earth rejoiced at the apparent death of the two witnesses (some of the first to become like Jesus).

because these two prophets[324] tormented[325] them that dwelt on the earth.

11 And after three days and a half[326] the Spirit of life[327] from God entered into them, and they stood[328] upon their feet;[329] and **mega** fear fell upon them which saw them.

12 And they heard a mega voice from heaven saying to them, **walk-up here.** And they **walked-up** to heaven in a cloud; and their enemies **looked-closely-at** them.

---

[324] The "two prophets" may symbolize the twofold prophetic Church walking in the spirit and power of Moses and Elijah. They also symbolizes two (fold) sons of golden olive oil that "supply the Spirit of Jesus" (the gold oil of the Holy Spirit) to the candlesticks (the Church)—Zechariah 4, Philippians 1:19). In Zechariah 4:2, the "bowl" that supplied the oil to the two olive trees is also defined as a "fountain." Hence, God's fountain of oil, supplies His oil to the two olive trees (also called the sons of oil). The sons of oil (the two olive trees) in turn supply the candlestick with the same gold oil of the Holy Spirit, through the conduits of the hands (see the Hebrew definitions for Zechariah 4:12 w/Acts 8:18 and Acts 19:6, etc.). Note that in Luke 4:18 Jesus calls "the Lord" He who "anoints" with the Spirit; therefore, oil is also a symbol of the Spirit. Do you have the eternal oil in your lamp (your body) as the 5 wise virgins (Matthew 25:1-13)? Being filled with the Holy Spirit and being refilled with the Holy Spirit is part of our inheritance and seal of God (Acts 2:1-21 w/Acts 2:38-39, Acts 19:2-6 w/Ephesians 1:13).

[325] Jesus and Paul were accused of something similar. In John 7:7, we learn that Jesus was hated; because he called the world evil; and in Acts 24:5 Paul was called a "pestilent."

[326] Contrast 1 Corinthians 15:4; God waited 3 ½ days to resurrect the two witnesses as opposed to 3 days in Jesus' resurrection, therefore, Jesus continues to have the "preeminence" in all things (Colossians 1:18).

[327] The Spirit of Life is for those "in Christ Jesus" (Romans 8:2)

[328] Resurrection of the "first-fruit Christ;" this is **not** the same as the resurrection of Christ (Jesus) the first-fruit—1 Corinthians 15:20-23.

[329] 2 Chronicles 3:13 and Ezekiel 37:20, similar phrase is used of the two cherubs made of olive trees and the army of the Israel of God. The two cherubs of olive trees stood in the middle of the Oracle (cherubs were 20 cubits wide, 10 cubits tall and 10 cubits back from front of Oracle (20x10x10=2,000 cubits (2,000 years from Jesus' ascension).

13 And **in that hour** was there a **mega** earthquake, and the tenth of the city[330] fell and in the earthquake were **killed names of-men** seven thousand; and the remnant was **in-fear**, and gave glory to the God of heaven.

14 The second woe is past; **be-perceiving** the third woe **is-coming shortly**.

15 And the seventh[331] angel **trumpeted**;[332] and there were mega voices in heaven, saying, the **kingdom** of this world **became of-our** Lord,[333] and of his Christ; and he shall reign[334] **into the ages of ages**.

16 And the twenty-four elders, **the-ones sitting** before God on their **thrones**, fell upon their faces,[335] and worshipped God,[336]

---

[330] This "city" is Mystery Babylon, **not** Jerusalem.

[331] The seventh trumpet is the last of the seven trumpets. There is no trumpet to sound after this trumpet. Therefore, this trumpet is also called the "last trumpet" in 1 Corinthians 15:52. It is also called the "trumpet of God" in 1 Thessalonians 4:16; because seven is the number of God, or God's rest. As it is written, "... He rested on the seventh day ..." (Genesis 2:2b).

[332] The angel prophesied the very event that occurred.

[333] Romans 4:13; 16; Hebrews 12:27; Daniel 7:22

[334] The millennium reign of Christ begins after the "Last" or 7th Trumpet. According to Paul the saints reigning with Christ is a corporate rule to come (1 Cor 4:8)

[335] Moses practiced the same thing during intercession (Numbers 16:14). We should do the same before our Great King and Father of spirits.

[336] The worship of God is their mode of operation and God seeks such worshippers (John 4:23-24).

17 Saying, we give you thanks, O Lord God Almighty, **which are, and was;**[337] because you have taken to you your **mega** power,[338] and have reigned.

18 And the nations were **grasping-angry,**[339] and your **grasping-anger** is come, and the season of the dead, that they should be judged,[340] and that you should give reward[341] to your servants the prophets, and to the saints, and them that fear your name, small and **mega**; and should **through-rotted** them which **through-rotting** the earth.[342]

---

[337] Note: in the Majority texts and in the Alexandrian texts, the phrase "the one coming" is not in the Greek as previously written in other verses in the book of Revelation (i.e. Revelation 1:4; Revelation 4:8). The phrase is now excluded from this point forward. This then begs the question, why was this phrase ("the one coming") not used in this verse? It appears that the Lord comes during the seventh trumpet, or the "last trumpet;" hence the exclusion of the phrase "the one coming." He can't be "the one coming," any longer if He comes during this trumpet.

[338] "Mega (great) power" is directly related to God's resurrection power (Acts 4:33); therefore, it is implied that resurrection occurred in His coming during this "trumpet of God" (the Seventh Trumpet), widely known as the "last trumpet."

[339] Compare the angry nations in Psalms 2:1-2 and Psalms 99:1.

[340] Translated as "called in question" (Acts 23:6; 24:21, KJV); "sentenced" (Acts 15:19, KJV); also linked to the dead being evangelized (1 Peter 4:6, 1 Peter 3:18-20)

[341] The rewards given out to the prophets, those who feared God and saints happened in reference to the 7th Trumpet, the season of the coming of the Lord Jesus (compare 1 Corinthians 4:5).

[342] Mystery Babylon used prostitution to corrupt—Revelation 19:2.

19 And the temple of God[343] was opened in heaven, and there was seen in his temple the Ark[344] **the Covenant**[345] **His Covenant**; and there were lightnings, and voices, and thunders, and an earthquake, and **mega** hail.

---

[343] There is a heavenly tabernacle (Hebrews 9:11-12); yet this also points to the temple of God, the Church who sits in heavenly places in Christ (1 Corinthians 3:17 w/Ephesians 2:6).

[344] If this is literal, this is the last place the Ark is seen. With that said, no man should attempt to rebuild the natural Ark here or in Israel. Jeremiah 3:16-18 said: "And it shall come to pass, when you be multiplied and increased in the land, in those days, says the LORD, they shall say no more, The ark of the covenant of the LORD; neither shall it come to mind: neither shall they remember it; neither shall they visit it; **neither shall that be done any more.** At that time they shall call Jerusalem the throne of the LORD; and all the nations shall be gathered unto it, to the name of the LORD, to Jerusalem: neither shall they walk any more after the imagination of their evil heart. In those days the house of Judah shall walk with the house of Israel, and they shall come together out of the land of the north to the land that I have given for an inheritance unto your fathers."

[345] The "Ark of the Covenant" is foremost a symbol of Jesus, the Christ, of the "New Covenant" and/or Jesus, the Christ of "the everlasting covenant;" the Ark seen **in** the temple points to Christ [the Ark] being seen **in** us [His temple]. Jesus is the hope of our glory. The phrase "there was seen in His Temple the Ark of the Covenant of Him" may have direct reference to Joshua 3:3-17 representing the Church "passing over" into the kingdom age through Jesus' everlasting covenant through which he also cut off sin all the way back to Adam's sin that was passed down to us. The "Covenant" also represents the 10 Commandments (see Rev 15).

CHAPTER 12

1 And there appeared a **mega** wonder in heaven; a woman[346] clothed with the sun[347] and the moon[348] under her feet and upon her head a crown of twelve stars.[349]

2 And she **in belly holding** cried, travailing in birth,[350] and **tormented to-produce**.[351]

---

[346] This woman is Zion (Isaiah 66:7-8). This woman is the Church, New Jerusalem (Ephesians 5:32 w/Ephesians 5:22-33, Revelation 21, etc.).

[347] The "woman clothed with the sun" points to the Church of Jesus being clothed with the armor of light, Jesus, the Christ, (Romans 13:12-14); or the light of Jesus' righteousness that heals us (Malachi 4:2).

[348] This may apply to the woman overcoming ceremonial legalistic holy days that are observed by some in the Church (Psalms 104:19, Galatians 4, Colossians 2). It also point to her overcoming the works of darkness through the "lesser light" of the moon light that was ordained to rule the night and darkness (Genesis 1:16(.

[349] Since, twelve stars are specified here, it appears to me that it relates to the 11 stars (Joseph's 11 brothers), plus 1 star (Joseph) that Joseph saw in a vision to represents the sons of Jacob who eventually became the 12 patriarchs of the 12 tribes of Israel. Thus, the 12 stars are symbolic of the Church being crowned with the 12 tribes of Israel. In other words, the Jewish sons of God will once again have significant roles in the Church as leaders and they will be like a crown to the Church as Peter, James, John, Paul, etc. were crowns to the early Church. The twelve starts may also represent the apostolic angels of the Church (Rev 1:19-20) who witnesses according to the "Beth Din" principle (twelve witnesses who through common law unanimously establish the truth that Jesus is the Christ, the Son of the living God).

[350] This can apply to a spiritual travailing in birth until Christ is formed in us, exemplified by her producing the "male mature-son" (Galatians 4:19).

[351] Conforming to the image of Jesus (producing Jesus in our lives) is not an easy task. It is experienced through birth pains. The Church will effectively be in torment until she produces having the image of Jesus (Galatians 4:19 w/Romans 8:29).

3 And there appeared another wonder in heaven; and behold a **mega fiery-red** dragon, having seven heads and ten horns, and seven crowns[352] upon his heads.[353]

4 And his tail[354] **dragged** the third of the stars of heaven[355], and did cast them to the earth; and the dragon stood before the woman **who-of-intending to-produce; to-eat-down** her child **whenever she-produced.**

---

[352] The seven heads (kings) of the beast are never crowned because Satan wears these crowns; hence he is the ruling spirit over the beast with its seven heads (see notes in Revelation 13 and Revelation 17).

[353] Satan is also a corporate entity; there is Beelzebub, the prince of demons; which Jesus defines as Satan (Beelzebub) of Satan (demons) –Matthew 12:24 w/Matthew 12:26.

[354] The dragon's "tail" is symbolic of the corporate false prophets of Satan that teach lies. According to Isaiah 9:15a "the prophet that teaches lies, he is the tail."

[355] According to Hebrews 11:12, these represent Abraham's seed (the Church made up of Jews and other ethnicities); these stars do not appear to be angels; since the "tail" represents false prophets that teach lies, the stars being dragged to the ground can represent persecution by lying on the seed or a falling away (the apostasy) caused by false prophets' convincing lies (1 Tim 4:1, 2 Thess 2).

5 And she **produced a son,**[356] **a male,**[357] **who is-intending to shepherd** all nations with a rod of iron;[358] and her child **is-snatched towards** God, and his throne.[359]

6 And the woman fled into the wilderness,[360] where she has a place **internally-prepared from** God that **they**[361]**-should-nourish** her there a thousand two hundred sixty days.[362]

---

[356] This is a corporate "son" made up of "many sons" also defined as a "nation" (holy nation) According to Isaiah 66:7-9.

[357] See Isaiah 66:7-7 where the "male" is explained.

[358] This phrase foremost was used for Jesus in Revelation 19:15. However, most of what applies to Jesus, the pattern Son, also applies to God's many sons (Revelation 12:5; 2:23); and according to Psalms 2:7-9, Revelation 2:23 is a sonship principle. David gathered the courage to declare what God said of him and the Messiah, "I will declare the decree: the LORD has said unto me, you are my Son; this day have I begotten you. 8Ask of me, and I shall give you the heathen for your inheritance, and the uttermost parts of the earth for your possession. 9You shall break them with a rod of iron; you shall break them in pieces like a potter's vessel."

[359] Their place "towards [God's] Throne, with God as conquering sons (Revelation 3:21). They being "seized" to God and his Throne can be both "in body" or "out of body" experience (2 Cor 12:2-4). This is he 30th (the number of maturity) God's or the Lamb of God's Throne is mentioned.

[360] Hosea 2:14-20

[361] I believe the "they" who will nourish this woman (the Church) is the male-child (the many sons) that she will produce. Isaiah 66:7-8 made it clear that Zion's (Jesus' wife) "male" who was born represents "her children (lit., her sons)." They will hear from God in His Throne and feed her with the principles of bread from heaven (principles of our Lord Jesus Christ)

[362] This is the same time period as the days of the two witness and written in this form (1,260 days) to distinguish it from being written as 42 months (man's (6) opposition against God (7)).

7 And there was war in heaven. Michael[363] and his angels fought[364] against the dragon; and the dragon fought and his angels.

8 And **not they-are-forceful**; neither was **a place**[365] **for him** found any more in heaven.

9 And the **mega** dragon was cast out, that **original** serpent,[366] called the Devil, and Satan, which **cause-to stray** the **whole habitable-house**; he was cast out into the earth, and his angels[367] were cast out with him.

10 And I heard a **mega** voice saying in heaven, now is come salvation, and **power,** and the kingdom of our God, and the

---

[363] According to the Talmud and 1 Enoch 20, there are seven angels that are before the Lord: there is Uriel, Raphael, Raguel, Michael, Saraqâêl, Gabriel, and Remiel. Here are the meanings of their names. Uriel, "fire of God;" Raphael, "healer of God;" Raguel, the shepherd or friend of God; Michael, "he who is like God;" Saraqâêl, "command of God;" Gabriel, "man (or mighty) of God;" and Remiel, "thunder of God." Michael, the archangel is found in the book of Daniel, Jude, and Revelation. Gabriel is found in Daniel and Luke. You may refer to my book titled *Angels and the Supernatural.*

[364] Archangels usually fight the ruling spirit that rules as the invisible princes of nations to make sure the desired changes of God take place in the heavenly and in the kingdoms of the earth (see Daniel 10:1 through Daniel 11:1). God is in total control!

[365] Satan has been displaced; he is displaced, and he shall continue to be displaced. One of the purposes of God "placing sons" (adopted) is to dispossess Satan from the place Satan usurped; the Scripture says don't give him place (topo); that is, since he likes to "place" himself among the sons of God (Job 1:6; 2:1); we are also commanded not to give him place (Ephesians 4:27).

[366] This is same "original serpent," the Devil, in the Eden; Satan was not speaking through a natural serpent in the Garden of Eden; he is the serpent that spoke, yes, the dragon is the original serpent (see also 2 Corinthians 11:3). Refer to my book titled *When the Lord Made the Tempter.*

[367] These are some of the "high things" (lit., high-bodies) that we are to also cast down (1 Corinthians 10:5).

authority of his Christ;[368] for the **categorizer**[369] of our brethren is cast down, which **categorized** them before our God day and night.

11 And they overcame him by the blood[370] of the Lamb and by the word of their testimony; and they loved not their **souls until** death.[371]

12 Therefore **rejoice**[372] you heavens, and you that **tabernacle** in them. Woe to the **dwellers** of the earth and of the sea![373] For the devil is come down to you, having **mega sacrifice-wrath**, because he **perceives** that he has but a **puny** time.[374]

13 And when the dragon saw that he was cast to the earth, he persecuted the woman **any-who**[375] **produced the male.**

14 And to the woman were given two wings of a **mega** eagle[376] that she might fly into the wilderness, into her

---

[368] The authority of Christ is "**all** authority in heaven and earth" that Jesus possesses (Matthew 28:18, Luke 10:17-18).

[369] Or, to sue at law; charge with offence

[370] Hebrews 12:24 (Jesus' blood speaks stronger things), I Samuel 17:1 (Ephes Dammin, the boundary of the blood drops the enemy cannot traverse).

[371] Jesus exemplified this same dedication "until death" as Paul stated in Philippians 2:1-8.

[372] This statement "rejoice you heavens" gives us a glimpse into the heavenly dimensions that were being adversely affected by Satan; and thus, they can now rejoice because Michael cast out Satan from the heavens into the earth.

[373] There are three dimensions in the book of Revelation, the heavens, the earth, and the sea (Dr. Kelley Varner).

[374] "Puny time" or "short time" is approximately the 3 ½ years of the beast's rule whom Satan will enthrone.

[375] The woman is symbolic of "any" in the Church "who" produce the male (Jesus) in their lives (compare Galatians 4:19). The woman is also called Zion (Isaiah 66, 1 Peter 2, Hebrews 12).

[376] This is God equipping her to be brought unto Himself (Exodus 19:4).

place,[377] where she is nourished for a **season**, and **seasons**, and half a **season**[378] from the face[379] of the serpent.

15 And the serpent cast out of his mouth water[380] as a flood after the woman, that he might cause her to be **river-burdened**.[381]

16 And the earth **ran-to the-cry**[382] **of-the** woman, and the earth opened her mouth,[383] and swallowed up the flood which the dragon cast out of his mouth.

---

[377] I believe "her place" is with God (Exodus 19:4).

[378] Season, seasons, half-a-season (or time, times, and half-a-time) can apply to the same time period as the 1,260 days and the 42 months (360 days (time), 720 days (times), 180 days (1/2 a time); see my other books for further development (*The Days of the Seventh Angel; The Last Hour, The First Hour, The 42nd Generation*).

[379] Cherubs have four faces in Ezekiel 1. The original serpent also implicitly appears to have four faces: the face of the serpent (Hebrew: hisser, to whisper (a spell), prognosticate)—the face of questioning God's intension through whispers; the face of the dragon (seeing one)—face of sight that accuses; the face of the Devil (throw-through)—the face that throws fire balls; and the face of Satan (Adversary)—the face of contests and opposing circumstances.

[380] Nothing clean comes out of the dragon (Revelation 16:13); so this is dirty water, or "dragon puke" (Kelley Varner).

[381] This explains the apparent burdens that sometimes overwhelm some of the saints.

[382] God has also made the earth to help His Church.

[383] Compared the similar judgment executed by Moses (Numbers 16:30-34)

17 And the dragon was **grasping-angry**[384] with the woman,[385] and went to make war[386] with the **remaining-ones** of her seed,[387] which **guard** the commandments of God,[388] and have the testimony of Jesus.[389]

CHAPTER 13

1 And I stood upon the sand of the sea and **perceived** a beast[390] **walk-up** out of the sea,[391] **having ten horns and**

---

[384] The rise of the two beasts in Revelation 13 came out of the anger of the serpent; that is, the first beast and the other beast was resurrected for the express purpose of "anger" killing "any-who produce the male" (Jesus) in their lives.

[385] The original serpent became angry with the woman, Mrs. Adam (Eve), when Adam chose her over him to be his help meet; and thus, the Devil tempted them beyond God's guidelines; and the original serpent became angry again when the woman, wife of the last Adam produced the man-child in the image of Jesus.

[386] He will make war, foremost; through the leopard beast (see Revelation 13:7).

[387] A phrase used by God in Genesis 3 that indicates the Devil's ultimate demise through the seed of a woman ("her seed). "Her seed" is Jesus and the rest of her seed are God's many sons who take on the image of the Son of God, Jesus (Gal 3:16; 3:23).

[388] This phrase may also be referencing the orthodox Jews according to the flesh who still observe the commandments of God, as it does to Christians.

[389] The testimony of Jesus is the spirit of prophesy. Therefore, the dragon will also persecute those who flow in the prophetic that testifies of Jesus and Jesus' resurrection (Revelation 19:10).

[390] One of the four Kingdoms explained by the prophet Daniel in Daniel 7, Daniel 8, Daniel 10, and Daniel 2

[391] The troubled sea of humanity, there are three (3) seas in the book of Revelation—the literal sea, the troubled sea of humanity, and the sea of glass mixed with fire.

seven heads, and upon his horns ten crowns,[392] and upon his heads the **names** of blasphemy.[393]

2 And the beast which I saw was like to a leopard,[394] and his feet were as of a bear,[395] and his mouth as the mouth of a lion;[396] and the dragon gave[397] him his power, and his **throne**,[398] and **mega** authority. [399]

---

[392] This means that the ten kings of Revelation 17 without crowns were ruling at the time of this beast's resurrection out of the sea of humanity, because they are now crowned; contrast Revelation 17 where the ten horns were not crowned because at that juncture "they received no kingdom as yet."

[393] The name of the beast is not necessarily a person's name; the name of the beast is blasphemy. Blasphemy, as defined in Mark 3, is to call the Holy Spirit of God an unclean spirit; the beast (spirit of Greece) will one day call genuine Christians evil; and the beast will call the Spirit of God who is in Christians an unclean spirit (Mark 3), etcetera.

[394] The leopard represents Greece or the spirit of Greece. Thus the leopard may point to the democratic philosophy of the Greeks with imperial aspirations like Alexander, the great (Daniel 7, Daniel 8, Daniel 10). Compare Jeremiah 5:6 to understand some of the traits of this beast kingdom that will rise again in the earth. With that said, here is a vision the Spirit of Lord Jesus showed me in 1992: It was a season of fasting. It was about the 9th day of the fast. My flesh was without strength as I sat on the sofa, and I saw and heard a voice say, **"The way is being made for the spirit of Greece."** I then heard a voice say, **"A great tragedy shall happen in America,"** as I heard the voice speak, **I saw a president standing upon a pile of rubble exactly as President Bush did after 9/11.** I then heard the voice say, **"After the tragedy, I will bring forth the Boy Scouts."**

[395] The excessive destruction of flesh (humanity) like the Persians (Daniel 7)

[396] The lion's mouth may point to the Babylonian systems (Daniel 3, Daniel 7); or the judiciary system of Rome (2 Timothy 4:17).

[397] Why did the dragon give the beast his power? The beast was a Satan worshipper (contrast Matthew 4:8-9); and he was given power and authority to persecute the sons of God (Rev 16:17-13:1).

[398] This includes, but is not limited to, the throne in Pergamos (Revelation 2:13) that is related to the throne of deep idolatrous worship and the throne that sanctions martyrdom of the saints. Pergamos is located in modern day Turkey.

[399] The mega authority is found in Revelation 13:7—authority over all nations, kindred, and tongues, also administered through the conquest of war.

3 And **I-perceived first**[400] of his heads as it were **butchered** to death; and his **plague of-the death** was **therapeutic**; and **marveled** the **whole earth behind** the beast.

4 And they worshipped the dragon which gave **authority** to the beast; and they worshipped the beast, saying, who like to the beast? Who is able to make war[401] with him?

5 And there was given to him a mouth speaking **mega** things and blasphemies; and **authority** was given to him to **make-war** forty-two months.

6 And he opened his mouth in blasphemy against God,[402] to blaspheme his name,[403] and his tabernacle,[404] them that **tabernacle** in heaven.

7 And it was given to him to make war with the saints,[405] and to overcome them; and **authority** was given him over all[406] kindred **and people,** and tongues, and nations.

---

[400] Since the leopard beast represents the kingdom of Greece and the spirit of Greece with its four heads in Daniel 7, the "first head" would represent Alexander, the Great and his philosophy. See notes for Revelation 17:13.

[401] Whenever the leopard beast (the spirit of Greece, democracy, imperialism, communism, royalties, etcetera that turns on true Christians) comes into its fullness, it will also be war machine used to exert "authority" over "all kindred, tongues and nations."

[402] Calling the Holy Spirit an unclean spirit (Mark 3), etcetera

[403] Calling Jesus' name unclean and Beelzebub (Mark 3)

[404] Calling the Church demonic and unclean (Mark 3)

[405] He made "war with the saints" fulfilling the purpose of Satan resurrecting this beast (Revelation 12:17a); every nation, through laws, etc. will one day turn against true believers of Jesus.

[406] The beast (the spirit of Greece) will exercise authority over kindred (families), tongues (over freedom of speech), and nations (ethnicities).

109

8 And all that dwell upon the earth shall worship him, whose names are not written in the Book of Life[407] of the Lamb slain from the foundation[408] of the world.

9 If any man has an ear, let him hear.[409]

10 If anyone has captivity,[410] he is going; if anyone in sword is-killing must himself in sword be-killed. Here is the **endurance** and the faith of the saints.[411]

---

[407] Here is an apparent absolute: the only way **not** to fall into the trap of worshipping the beast is to be written in the Book of Life—being written in the Book of Life can only come through Jesus, the Son of the one true God and Father; the Father of our Lord Jesus Christ; believers "are come to … the Church of the 'firstborns' which are registered in heaven" (Hebrews 12:22-24).

[408] 1 Peter 1:20 w/Hebrews 9:26—Jesus Christ dying for us in Spirit from the beginning and fulfilled literally was kept secret until Christ came almost 2000 years ago (see also Matthew 13:35).

[409] Sine he references "any man that has an ear," then the understanding ("hearing") being conveyed can be understood by anyone with an ear.

[410] A reference to Jeremiah 15:1-4 with regards to King Manasseh's wickedness and the judgments (beast's captivity and mystery Babylon's captivity).

[411] The "faith of the saints" may reference "those who keep ..the faith of Jesus," the "faith of the Son of God" (Rev 14:11-12, Gal 2:20). Note: there is a difference between faint "in" Jesus and the faith "of" Jesus, which appears to be a willingness to die for the heavenly Father, if necessary.

11 And **I-perceived** another beast[412] **walking-up** out of the earth; and he had two[413] horns like a lamb,[414] and he spoke[415] as a dragon.

12 And he **does** all the **authority** of the first beast before him and makes the earth[416] and them which dwell **in her** to

---

[412] This "another beast" is the Antichrist and/or the spirit of antichrist. I John 4:1-3 calls the spirit of antichrist "false prophets;" Revelation 16:13 and Revelation 19:20 calls this "another beast" the "false prophet." Again, the Antichrist is **not** the first beast. The Antichrist is the false prophet and his many false prophets who propagates the leopard beast. 1 John 2 also defines antichrists (plural) as people who are deceived to permanently leave Christ Jesus and His Church. Please see my other titles for further development: *The False Prophet, Alias, Another Beast, Son of Man Prophesy against the False Prophets, and The Dragon's Tail (The Many False Prophets)*. The following is a vison the Lord gave me in the early 1990s: My wife and I were in a season of intensified prayer. On this particular morning, we prayed through the night. After the intensified prayer, we laid down to get some sleep; however, immediately I was in a vision. In the vision, I saw a red (komodo-like) dragon and I in the heat of a battle. I could see that I wrestled this red dragon out of the sky to the ground. I then descended from the heavenly sphere to see what became of the dragon. I was aware that my clothes were ripped up as a result of being engaged in intensified fighting against the red dragon. As I was descending, the red dragon began to pursue me, again. I ascended again to the heavens as he pursued me. As he was pursuing me, I turned toward him to fight, and fire came out of my mouth and devoured him (Compare Revelation 11:5, Jeremiah 23:29). The beast then fell, again, to the ground as dead, however he was not. As I descended from the heavenly, I saw my wife going to throw on the beast some sort of solid foam. In the vision, my wife was strong in appearance; and the plats of her hair was long and sturdy in appearance. As she was about to approach the dragon to assess the condition of the red dragon, I called out to her and said, "He is not dead as he may appear." As I said this to my wife, the beast stood up; and I could see him in plain view. To my amazement, though, the great red dragon had mutated into an animal-man; that is, his appearance was that of a man (he resembled a very prominent prophet), but he had two huge horns like a male lamb. The horns started from his temple curling back towards his ears, as the appearance of a ram with great horns. At this sight, the vision ended. Revelation 13:11 describes a beast that has two horns like a lamb; however, it speaks like a dragon. This same "another beast" is also called "the false prophet" in Revelation 16:13 and Revelation 19:20. It is also worthy to note that Satan is

worship the **before-most** beast whose **plague of-death** was **therapeutic**.

13 And he does mega **signs**,[417] so that he makes fire[418] come down from heaven on the earth in the sight of men.[419]

---

called a fiery red dragon; hence this "another beast" that speaks "as" a dragon is in reality a dragon. "As," in Revelation 13:11, is the Greek word "hos" which is defined as "who," "which," "what," and "that." Hence, "he 'who' is a dragon," speaks "what," "as a dragon."

[413] Horn is usually symbolic of a kingdom; hence the two horns may point to a religious system that claims both secular kingdom and religious kingdom. Is this the Vatican? Is this Islam? Is this Mormonism? The two horns may also point to the limited false witness as opposed to the seven horns of the true Lamb of God (Revelation 5). Horns is also a symbol of power, in this case his horn is satanic power.

[414] Jesus used the same metaphor in Matthew 7:15-23 of false prophets who come in sheep clothing, but they are wolves on the inside. See the subtitle "A Dragon-A Man with Two Horns like a Lamb" in "Section #3 concerning a vision I had.

[415] He spoke like a dragon, which can mean that he is an accuser, and he persecutes by categorizing (Revelation 12:10); dragons also questions God's integrity and purpose (Genesis 3:1-5).

[416] His deception is so convincing that it even deceives the earth that once helped the Church in Revelation 12 (not just the people of the earth, but the earth herself will also be deceived). The groaning creation will think that this beast is one of God's sons (Romans 8:19; 22).

[417] Luke 21:11; Matthew 24:24; 2 Thessalonians 2:1-11

[418] Calling down fire from heaven is now contrary to the operations of God, according to Jesus in Luke 9:54-56. The false prophet may also be attempting to copy Elijah in order to deceive. However, God's fire is now to come out of the mouth of God's true prophets (Revelation 11:5, Jeremiah 5:14).

[419] Public boasting (Matthew 6:1); contrast Jesus' low key mode of operation in Mark 7:36.

112

14 And **it-strays**[420] **my-own-people**[421] the-ones dwelling on the earth by those **signs** which **he-was-given** to do in the sight of the beast; saying to them that dwell on the earth, that they should make an image to[422] the beast, which had the **plague** by a sword, and did live.[423]

15 And **he was-given to-give spirit**[424] to the image of the beast that the image of the beast should both speak,[425] and

---

[420] This phrase is present tense in the Greek text, which may point to the fact that the Jews (his own people) were deceived by the beast of that day (Rome); and thus took on the spirit-image (antichrist spirit) of Rome. Or does this mean that Israel will forsake God of Jesus, Abraham, Isaac, and Jacob (the same God and Father of the Church) "theocratic rule" and embrace the spirit of Greece democratic principles?

[421] Or "my-own," the people of John, the Jews, will be deceived by this "Antichrist" (lit., instead of Christ). The Jews, who rejected Christ Jesus, were apparently deceived by the antichrist spirit and it appears that the Jews will again be deceived by the Antichrist and its spirit. Or does "my-own" point to Church people who will be deceived by this false prophets and hence the spirit of the false prophet in the many false prophets.

[422] Note: This is an image "to" the beast, not just a manmade image "of" the beast. Contrast Jesus who was the image of the invisible God (Colossians 1:15); hence making an image to the beast can be those who take on the image of the spirit behind the beast.

[423] This appears to be the resurrection of the kingdom of Greece or the resurrection of the spiritual prince of Greece. The first head of Greece, as the leopard kingdom, was Alexander, the Great; who was ruled by the "prince of Greece" or the "demon goat" of Greece (Daniel 7; Daniel 8; Daniel 10). In fact, in Daniel 8: "demon goat" is literally "demon she-goat," which may also point to Alexander's known bisexuality. See the notes for Revelation 17:13 for additional development.

[424] Pseudo life from an unclean spirit (Revelation 16:13); and yes, Satan will be using all signs, wonders, and powers of falsehood to deceive people (2 Thessalonians 2:7-12) to take the name, number, and mark of the beast.

[425] The false prophet's limited spirit could only make the image speak. However, God did not allow this spirit to cause hearing, seeing, and walking (compare Revelation 9:20).

113

make as many as would not worship the image of the beast should be killed.[426]

16 And he **makes** all, both small and **mega**, rich, and poor, free and bond, to **give themselves**[427] an **engraving**[428] **on** their **right,** or **on** their foreheads.[429]

---

[426] There will be a time in the earth where the spirit of Greece (the leopard) with the philosophy of Greece (absolute democracy) will use death as a means to control the populous by the changing of the current freedoms in/through democratic laws to legislate total submission to the beast and its system (compare Daniel 7:25, etc.).

[427] Some people "give themselves" the "mark" of the beast. According to Acts 17:29, the mark is also imprinted by "technology;" that is "art" (KJV) is the Greek word "technes" from where we get the English word technology, technique, tech, etc.); and the mark is also imprinted by "internal-anger" ("devices" (KJV) , a compound Greek word of "en" (in) and "thumos" (wrath, kill-wrath, sacrifice-wrath, hot-wrath)).

[428] Greek: "chragma" (mark) is first used by Sophocles of a "serpent's bite;" and in this case a "beast's" bite. "Charagma" according to Vines Dictionary is **"akin"** to the Greek word "charakter." A "charakter" is the engraver (tool or person) that produced the "chragma," the engraving. Since, beast kings and kingdoms exist and will exist in every age until Jesus eradicate the beasts, the mark of the beast also existed in every age. In other words, the mark of the beast is a present reality, and not just a future event; and it is to be rejected by all true believers, even if it means until death.

[429] A compound of two Greek words: "meta" (change, beyond, middle, with) and "ops" (eyes), to change the way one sees (eyes), or beyond the eyes (what is beyond forehead? the mind); forehead points to the way one sees and thinks; and therefore the mark of the beast on the forehead is the false prophet's ("another beast") method of changing the deceived to see and think like the beast.

17 And that no man[430] **may-be-able to-redeem** or sell, **if not the-one having** the **engraving,**[431] the name[432] of the beast, or the number[433] of his name.

18 Here is wisdom.[434] Let him that has understanding[435] count the number of the beast; **it is the number because**[436] **of a man**; and his number six-hundred sixty, six.[437]

---

[430] Will Islamic terrorism (in the natural) drive the implementation of implanted "technology" so that "no man (human)" will be able to do commerce without being tracked in an effort to curb terrorism? That is, will terrorism, etc. be the excuse to implement worldwide use of the mark of the beast, with the real reason related to Revelation 12:17? Or will lawlessness in humanity be used as a guise to implement the mark of the beast?

[431] The mark ("charagma") of the beast is only used eight (8) times in the book of Revelation and once (1) in Acts 17:29. The engraving (mark) of his name is blasphemy (Revelation 14:11). Acts 17:29 indicates that the mark of the beast is imparted through "tech" being used the wrong way and man's "in-wrath" (internal sacrifice or kill-wrath). According to Hebrews 12:4, this internal-sacrifice-wrath ("intent") can be discerned by the Word of God who is in us. According to Jesus this internal-sacrifice-wrath ("thoughts") is also linked to blasphemy and wickedness that hurts others (Matthew 9:4; 12:25).

[432] The name of the beast is blasphemy (Revelation 13:1).

[433] The number of the beast is 666, the number of man's blasphemy against God.

[434] Jesus is made unto us Wisdom and the Wisdom of God (1 Corinthians 1:24; 30); hence only the Christian minds that hold Jesus (having the mind of Christ (1 Corinthians 2:16)) can fully understand (recognize) the number of the beast so as **not** to take the number, mark of name of the beast.

[435] Literally "mind." What mind? The minds of God's people that have the Wisdom of Christ in them! "Christ Jesus ... is made unto us wisdom" (see 1 Corinthians 1:30).

[436] The number 666 is a number **"because"** (Greek "gar") of man; it is not necessarily a number for man. In other words, man is the **"cause"** of this number.

[437] The "Textus Receptus" use letters for the number of the beast (666); χ—600-ζ—60—ς-6; and for further understanding, the reader may also refer to my Book titled, *The Numbers of God*, the chapters titled "6" and "666."

CHAPTER 14

1 And **I-perceived** and **be-perceiving 'the'** Lamb stood on the mount Zion,[438] and with him a hundred forty-four[439] thousand, having his name and his Father's[440] name written[441] on their foreheads.[442]

2 And I heard a voice from heaven, as the voice of many waters, and as the voice of a **mega** thunder; and I heard the voice of harpers harping with their harps.

---

[438] Mount Zion is the Church of Jesus made up of Jesus the Living Stone and his holy priesthood also called living stones (1 Peter 2: 4-6); and she will have sons who are called "males" (Rev 12:1-5, Isaiah 66:7-10). These males are also inclusive of the 144,00 referenced in Reve 14:1-5)

[439] 144 is the symbolic number of the measure of the Man Jesus (Revelation 21:17 w/Ephesians 4:13, etc.). The definition of becoming a "mature" man is love (1 Corinthians 13). These may also represent the firstfruit of Israel who accepted Jesus before Acts 8:1-4 occurred (spreading the gospel to the nations). These may also represent the firstfruit believers of God's harvest throughout the ages (James 1:1; 1:18; Rom 16:5). See footnotes below for "firstfruit." The 144,000 may also reference the first fruit of every kindred, tougue, people and nation (Rev 5:9; Rev 14:3).

[440] The mystery of God is the mystery of Jesus Christ as the Son of God and God being the Father of the Son and His many sons (Colossians 2:2; Revelation 10:7).

[441] The Father's and the Lamb's name was written on them through the ink of the Spirit of the living God (2 Corinthians 3:3).

[442] A compound of two Greek words: "meta" (change, beyond, middle, with) and "ops" (eyes), to change the way one sees (eyes), or beyond the eyes (what is beyond forehead? the mind); and therefore the seal of God gives the ability to see like the Father and think like Jesus (1 Corinthians 2:16, Philippians 2:5-7).

3 And **they-are-singing as**[443] a new song[444] before the throne, and before the four **living-things**, and the elders; and no man could **disciple**[445] that song **if-not** the hundred forty-four thousand, which were redeemed from the earth.

4 These are they which were not **soiled** with women;[446] for they are virgins.[447] These are they which follow the Lamb whithersoever he goes. These were redeemed **by Jesus** from among **the** men,[448] the **firstfruit**[449] to God and to the Lamb.

---

[443] The Alexandrian text indicate that "they sang 'as' a new song." In other words, they became the song, because they became disciples of the song of the Lord (see notes directly below).

[444] Is this the "new song" of Revelation 5:9-10? A "new song" is a spontaneous song for the Lord and is sung by the Lord Jesus in us (Hebrews 2:12; Colossians 3:16). This may also be the Song of Solomon personified.

[445] According to Vines dictionary the Greek word "manthano" is "**akin** to mathetes, **"a disciple").**" Not only did they learn the song, but they also became disciples of the song by practicing (living) what they sang.

[446] The city, Jerusalem is called a woman; and the city Babylon (including her daughters) is also called a woman; hence the women in this verse appear to be referring to the religious entities.

[447] Christians in Christ are called virgins (2 Corinthians 11:1-2); so it appears that this may relate to virgins who did not defile themselves with Mystery Babylon and her daughters that Babylon mothers (Revelation 17:5); remember religion has "wings" that appear "pious" and this religious system was founded in a place called Shinar (another name for Babylon) (see Hebrew definition for "stork" in the study of "Shinar" in Zechariah 5:5-11); therefore some may be deceived by outward piousness into following a system that corrupts virginity (purity in body and spirit).

[448] These being redeemed from among "the men," may imply that they were redeemed from among those who reached the stature of "the mature man" in Ephesians 4:13. A manure man is a man of love (1 Corinthians 13).

[449] First, this applies to the firstfruit Jews that were saved from the days of John, the Baptist until God turned from the Jews to the Gentiles in Acts 13:46. The Jews in those days were called "some" of Jesus' first-fruit according to James 1:18. In James 1:18, the phrase "a kind of firstfruits" (KJV), literally reads "**some** of the firstfruit...." Second, these can also apply to the firstfruit true Jews (the Church according to Paul in Romans 2:28-29), or the firstfruit of the Israel of God (Romans

5 And in their mouth was found no **falsehood**; for they are without fault.

6 And I saw another[450] angel fly in the **mid-heaven**, having the everlasting gospel to **evangelize** them that dwell on the earth, and to every nation,[451] and kindred, and tongue, and people,[452]

7 Saying with a **mega** voice, fear God,[453] and give glory to him; for the hour of his judgment is come; and worship him that made heaven, and earth, and the sea, and the fountains of waters.

8 And there followed another angel, saying, **Babylon the mega is fallen she has** made all nations drink of the wine of the **sacrifice-wrath** of her **prostitution**.

9:6-9 w/Galatians 6:15-17). The "Israel of God" (Galatians 6:16) are true believer to be differentiated from Israel "according to the flesh" (Romans 9:1; Romans 1: 6-9).

[450] Compare Luke 9:52, James 2:25 and Luke 7:27, which shows that angels also refer to God's apostles and prophets.

[451] As is the pattern, the turn came for the gospel to be preached to the Gentiles after the first-fruit remnant of the Jews were sealed and saved (Revelation 7:9 w/Revelation 7:1-8; Revelation 14:6 w/Revelation 14:1-5).

[452] This preaching of the everlasting gospel to every nation, kindred, tongue, and people was in **opposition** to Mystery Babylon's seat in these same areas (Revelation 17:15); and hence her killing of the saints as indicated in Revelation 17:6.

[453] The "everlasting gospel is a message that emphasizes the fear of God, and the glorifying of God as it relates to His creative power.

9 And the third angel followed them, saying with a **mega** voice, if any man worships the beast and his image, and **taking**[454] **engraving**[455] **on** his forehead, or **on** his hand.

10 The same shall drink of the wine of the **sacrifice-wrath** of God, which is **blended un-held**[456] into the cup of his **grasping-anger**; and he shall be tormented with fire and **God-sulfur-lightning** in the presence of the holy angels, and in the presence of the Lamb.

11 And the smoke of their torment **walk-up into the ages of ages**; and they have no rest[457] day or night, who worship the beast and his image, and whosoever **takes** the **engraving** of his name.

12 Here is the **endurance** of the saints **keeping** the commandments of God, and the faith of Jesus.[458]

---

[454] Remember the mark was offered in Revelation 13:16, so they had a choice not to take the mark of the beast.

[455] The beast's mark is engraved in people by "tech" and their "internal-anger" according to Acts 17:26, the only other place where "charagma" is used other than the book of Revelation. Note that the apostle Paul also used "tech" in a positive application in Acts 18:3; so Paul was not against all technology. With that said, the ten toes (ten kings) in Daniel 2 will mix iron (technology) with clay (humans). Does this point to technology (metals) being implanted in or on humans? I must also note that those who have the Word of God in them will be able to discern ("be critical") of the "intent" (internal-anger) and "'mind' of the heart." Hence, true believers should not be deceived to take the mark of the beast.

[456] Greek: "akratos" (un-hold, not held), i.e., undiluted with water

[457] I have met many people who can't "rest" because of the satanic things they have practiced and the beastly images they have adopted as their own. It seems that a few people I have met who have dabbled in satanic activities are always tormented and restless as they journey out of the effects of former practices.

[458] The faith of Jesus is the faith to do the commandments of the Father even if it means death. Compare 2 Timothy 4:6-7 which documented Paul "fought" the "good fight" of faith. See also Galatians 2:2 and Revelation 13:10.

13 And I heard a voice from heaven saying to me, write, blessed the dead who die in the Lord from now; yes, says the Spirit that they may **up-pause** from their **weariness**; and their **acts** do follow them.[459]

14 And **I-perceived**, and **be-perceiving** a white cloud, and upon the cloud **sitting** like to the Son of man,[460] having on his head a golden crown, and in his hand a **keen gathering-hook**.

15 And another angel came out of the temple, crying with a mega voice to him **sitting** on the cloud, **send** in your **gathering-hook**, and reap; for the time is come to reap; for the harvest of the earth is **withered**.[461]

16 And he **sitting** on the cloud[462] **sends** in his **gathering-hook** on the earth; and the earth was reaped.

17 And another angel[463] came out of the temple, which is in heaven, he also having a **keen gathering-hook**.

---

[459] Even in death, the works of the saints do follow them. Remember Abel whose work followed him after death, in that even though he was dead, his blood yet speaks (Hebrews 11:4). The voices of Moses and the prophets are still heard even though they are dead (Acts 13:27; Acts 15:21).

[460] It takes the Church of Jesus Christ becoming like the son of man (Jesus) to reap the harvest; as opposed to the "messenger" who gathered the ones who will be thrown into the winepress of the wrath of God. In other words, we harvest more affectively when be become like the Son of man who walked in compassion, mercy, love, etc.

[461] Evangelism is withered, and it will take Jesus and those who become like him to reap the harvest.

[462] This is a metaphor that was instituted by Jesus concerning Him and His Church. The cloud can be symbolic of people (Hebrews 12:1, Jude 1:12, 2 Peter 2:17); Jesus said he would come **"on"** clouds, **"with"** cloud and **"in"** clouds (Matthew 24:30, Matthew 26:64, Mark 13:26, Mark 14:62, Luke 21:27).

[463] Note: This angel is not identified as the "Son of man." Hence, this angel functions differently. In other words, the use of the "Son of Man" implies Jesus' compassion.

18 And another angel **out-came out-of**[464] the altar,[465] which had **authority** over fire;[466] and cried with a loud cry to him[467] that had the **keen gathering-hook**,[468] saying, **send** in your **keen gathering-hook**, and gather the clusters of the vine of the earth;[469] for her grapes are **pointed-ripe.**[470]

---

[464] Intercessors (judges) live in the cramped place of the altar of incense (the restricted place of prayer). This messenger was apparently in the altar in order to hear the directive voice of the altar (Revelation 9:13, Revelation 16: 7).

[465] It is usually out of the place of the altar of incense (prayer) that prophetic directions usually come.

[466] This is the fire that is used to mix with the incense of prayer to provide protection for the priests of God (Revelation 8:5, Leviticus 16:12-13).

[467] Sometimes some of God's messengers don't have the faith to move until another messenger provides prophetic directives as encouragement to perform the will of God.

[468] I believe "keen gathering hook" points to the keen sight and knowing of apostolic and prophetic ministries as Jesus employed in John 4. Jesus used the **keen prophetic** (specific prophecy) to harvest the woman who had six men; and she in turn became part of the process to harvest the men of Samaria (John 4:17-19; 29; 35).

[469] There are two kinds of vines, one that crawls down to the earth (descending life of death) and one that climbs up (ascending life of Jesus). "The vine of the earth" (descending ones) whose grapes will be squeezed until obedience to the Lord is realized.

[470] This is the Greek "akme" (acme), a point, an edge, to be at the prime.

19 And the angel **sends**[471] in his **gathering-hook** into the earth, and gathered the vine of the earth, and cast into the **mega** winepress[472] of the **sacrifice-wrath**[473] of God.

20 And the winepress was trodden without the city,[474] and blood[475] came out of the winepress, **until** the horses'[476] bridles,[477] **from** a thousand six hundred[478] **stadiums**.[479]

---

[471] He listened to the prophetic directive of his peer who came from the narrow place of the altar. Today, some of God's preachers are so resistant to prophetic directives from their fellow peers, the peers who live in a narrow place of constant sufferings, financial challenges, reproaches, etc. That is, some prophetic preachers are marginalized because of their lack of financial clouts, and constant suffering for/through the gospel. These things ought not to be so.

[472] Winepress is used to press juice out of grapes; and thus Jesus will use this to press things out of those who are thrown into it. Jesus will tread the wine press alone and His garment will be made red (Isaiah 63:2-3; Revelation 19:13 w/19:15).

[473] Sacrifice-wrath does not necessarily mean death to condemnation. The root word for this word (wrath) is used in Acts 10:13 and is translated as "kill" in reference to God saving the gentiles by Peter "killing" and "eating" the "sacrifice" that God presented to him in a vision. "Kill" as translated in the King James Version in Acts 10:13, is defined as "sacrifice," the root word for "wrath;" hence "sacrifice-wrath" does not always point to literal death.

[474] "Without the city" is a place of suffering reproach for Jesus (Hebrews 13:11-13).

[475] Blood can point to wickedness Joel 3:12-14; this is the blood (wickedness) of the grapes that were pressed out of those thrown into the winepress.

[476] The horse of the Lord (Revelation 19:11 w/19:15) who alone qualifies to do the pressing; and the horses of them who follow Jesus when the blood of those who are being pressed flows outside the press (Revelation 19:14)

[477] The blood reaching the horses' bridles points to those in the winepress of the wrath of God who will be pressed until wickedness (blood) comes out that "they may obey" God (James 3:3).

[478] The number sixteen can be symbolic of the "completion" of cleansing (2 Chronicles 29:17); hence 1600 can be symbolic of cleansing accomplished in the places where 100-fold gospel is being preached.

CHAPTER 15

1 And **I-perceived** another sign in heaven, **mega** and marvelous, seven angels[480] having the seven last plagues; for in them is filled up the **sacrifice-wrath**[481] of God.

2 And I saw as it were a sea[482] of glass **mixed** with fire;[483] and them[484] that **overcame**[485] **out-of** the beast, and **out-of** his

---

[479] Stadiums represents the races (the places where the action of running occurs, the preaching the gospel—1 Corinthians 9:24-27, Galatians 2:2, etc.; there are stadiums (ministries who preach the gospel) in which some will have wickedness pressed out of them through the pressure of the Lord's horse.

[480] These angels are men (prophets).—Revelation 22:8-9

[481] According to Revelation 16:19, it appears that "orge" ("grasping-anger") is the "source" (genitive case) of "thumos" ("sacrifice-wrath"); that is, "sacrifice-wrath" was birthed out of "grasping-anger." In Revelation 16:19 it reads: "...the wine of-the 'thumos' of-the 'orge' of Him." Thus, the sacrifice-wrath (the bowls of wrath) that is referenced in Revelation 15:1 may be judgments that transformed progressively from "orge" to "thumos" during the seventh trumpet; that is, since the seventh trumpet manifested the "orge" (grasping-anger) of God, "orge" in turn becomes the source of God's "thumos" (kill-wrath), since some still refuse to repent.

[482] Symbolized by Solomon's "molten ("hard," "fused") sea" (2 Chronicles 4:2)

[483] Jesus is to baptize us with the Holy Spirit and fire; all were baptized unto Moses in the sea (I Corinthians 10:2, Exodus 15); believers will be baptized in the sea mixed with fire unto Jesus who baptizes us with/in fire (Matthew 3:11)

[484] The "them" are those who were not a people of God but were delivered to become "priests unto God." The sea is for the "priests to wash in." (1 Peter 2:9-10, 2 Chronicles 4:6, Revelation 5:10; Revelation 20:4-6)

[485] According to 2 Chronicles 4:5, complete "conquest" occurred at 3,000 baths (3,000 years) from Christ's resurrection. According to the circumference of the sea (30 cubits) multiplied by thickness of the brim (a "span" (David's life "span" was 70 years (Psalms 39:9)), and according to the circumference of the sea when its filled only to 2,000 baths (~20 cubits attained by ratio), the washing of the priesthood, from the influence of the beast, appears to occur from the days of Wycliffe (~20 x 70=~1400) and may consummate in 2,100 (70 x 30=2,100).

image **and out-of**[486] the number of his name,[487] stand on the sea of glass, having the harps of God.

3 And they sing the song of Moses[488] the servant of God, and the song of the Lamb,[489] saying, **mega** and marvelous your works, Lord God Almighty; just and true your ways, you King of **nations**.

4 Who shall not fear you, Lord, and glorify your name? For **only-you benign**[490] for all nations shall **arrive** and worship before you; for your **righteousness** are made manifest.[491]

---

[486] As Pharaoh and his 600 chariots were destroyed in the "Red Sea" (or literally, "termination sea", or "sea (of) termination." In Exodus 15, "Red" is the same Hebrew word for "termination" (סוף (SWPh)); it is also defined as conclusion and end. So likewise, God will end the chase of the beast, its name, its worship, and its image against these through baptism in the sea of glass mixed with fire unto Jesus. In other words, baptism in the sea of fire is the place where the influence of the beast is terminated, as Pharaoh and his army was terminated in the end sea. This principle of our enemy (Satan) and our past being cut off at baptism also applies when we get baptized by water into Jesus Christ.

[487] **Note:** In all of the Greek texts, the Majority Texts, the Alexandrian Text, (these are the oldest texts) there is no mention of victory out of the "mark" of the beast, except in the Received Text (not as old as the other texts). In other words, it appears that victory out of various aspects of the beast can be attained; however, once the mark or engraving of the beast is imprinted, there does not seem to be a way out of the mark and/or worshipping of the beast.

[488] This song of Moses seems to coincide with the song of Exodus 15 after God ended Pharaoh's chase in the Red (Termination) Sea, as God ends the beast's chase in the sea of glass mixed with fire.

[489] The song of the Lamb is the words of this verse and verse 4 (Revelation 15:3-4).

[490] Lit., Only Right (intrinsically) One, or Only Holy One

[491] The reason for their salvation is that the "righteous acts" of the Lamb were manifested as He manifested His righteousness for all others who have accepted Jesus' righteousness and righteous-acts (Romans 3:21-26; Romans 8:1-4). God is not prejudiced, and He made no difference among those in Revelation 15:2 that were delivered from the beast—see Romans 3:22.

5 And after that **I-perceived**, and, **be-perceiving,** the temple of the tabernacle of the testimony[492] in heaven was opened.

6 And the seven angels[493] came out of the temple, having the seven plagues, clothed in pure and white linen,[494] and having their **chest belted**[495] with golden **pocket-belt**.

7 And one of the four **living-things**[496] gave to the seven angels, seven golden **bowls** full of the **sacrifice-wrath** of God, who lives **into the ages of ages**.

---

[492] "The Testimony" represents, the Spirit of prophecy, the witness of the Lord Jesus (Rev 19:10); and "The Testimony" also represents "the Testimony," the Ten Commandments" placed in the Ark of the Covenant, "the Ark of the Testimony" (Deut. 9:11-15, Ex 32:15, Ex 39:35). God conversation with the 7 angels having the 7 last plagues relative to the Covenant of His Ten Commands (the Testimony) and the Lord Jesus (the Testimony) that was being rejected in the world (Compare God's plagues on humanity because of some of the Ten Commandments that were being breached in Rev 9:20-21 w/Rev 9:13-21). The 7 last plagues is related to, but not limited to, God's Covenant of "the Testimony" being excessively breached by humanity even though God's laws are written on their hearts (Rom 2:14-15). For example, breaching of God's first Commandment is judges in Rev 16:1-2, etc.

[493] According to Revelation Rev 21:9 w/Rev 22:8 8, Revelation 19:10, and so on, these angels are prophets. John's fellow servants and they are also of the royal priesthood (Jesus' Melchizedek order). Priest are the only ones allowed to do work related to God's temple. The Church must remember that she is a royal priesthood of Jesus' Melchizedek order; and if that is understood, the book of Revelation is filled with the function of Jesus our Great-High Priest and His priests administering the priesthood, seen in pictures or signs like "the temple of God" the golden altar, the seven lampstands, priests in their linen garments with the belts, the Ark of the Covenant, God's Throne, the Mercyseat, and so on.

[494] Fine line equals righteous-acts of the saints (Rev 19:7). These angels are saints, prophets, priests

[495] Belts are representative of strength (Isaiah 22:21). These prophets-priests were strengthened to administer the plagues due to the plagues harshness.

[496] One of God's seraph participating in the final distribution of the bowls of wrath.

8 And the temple[497] was filled with smoke from the glory of God, and from his power;[498] and **none** was able to enter into the temple, until the seven plagues of the seven angels were **finished**.

CHAPTER 16

1 And I heard a mega voice out of the temple saying to the seven angels, Go your ways, and pour out the **seven bowls**[499] of the **sacrifice-wrath**[500] of God **into** the earth.

2 And the first went and poured out his **bowl upon** the earth; and **became bad** and **hurtful ulcers**[501] **into** the men which had the **engraving** of the beast and them which worshipped his image.

3 And the second angel poured out his **bowl into** the sea; and it became as the blood of a **dead-one**[502] and every living soul[503] died in the sea.

---

[497] Is this the temple in heaven (Revelation 15:5) or the temple of His body (the Church which is also in heaven) (1 Corinthians 6:19 w/Ephesians 2:6)? The answer is, yes! This temple in heaven represents both the Body of Christ and the literal temple in heaven.

[498] This smoke of God's power may be linked to the preaching of the cross (see Romans 1:17, 1 Corinthians 1:18). Or no movement into the temple allowed during these plagues (contrast Numbers 10:11-13)

[499] Bowls full of God's sacrifice-wrath in liquid form

[500] The Word of God teaches that the "orge" (grasping-anger) is the "genitive case" or "source" of "thumos" (sacrifice-wrath)—Revelation 16:19, etc.

[501] Ulcers can occur in humans that take on the mark of the beast and those who worship the beast. With that said how many of us have things in our bodies from practices we participated in while under the beast system of the world before the Lord delivered us?

[502] No more life in the literal sea or the sea of humanity

[503] The first Adam was made a "living soul;" and therefore in conjunction with its literal meaning, it may also point to the deaths of people who refuse to give up the

4 And the third angel poured out his **bowl** upon the rivers and fountains of waters; and they became blood.

5 And I heard the angel of the waters say, you are righteous, who are, and was, and **the benign**,[504] because you have judged these.

6 For they have shed the blood[505] of saints and prophets, and you have given them blood to drink; for they are worthy.

7 And I heard the sacrifice-place say,[506] even so, Lord God Almighty, true, and righteous your judgments.

8 And the fourth angel poured out his **bowl** upon the sun; and **it-was-given** to him to scorch men with fire.

9 And men were scorched with mega heat,[507] and blasphemed[508] the name of God, which has **authority** over these plagues; and not **they-change-mind** to give him glory.

Adamic nature (the soul). The soul is linked to what people eat, drink, and wear, a person's goods, etc. (Matthew 6). Jesus asked us to lay down our soul that we may gain it. In (Matthew 16:25, Jesus said, "… whoever will save his 'soul' shall lose it; and whoever will lose his 'soul' for my sake shall find it."

[504] Right (intrinsically) One, or Holy One

[505] As indicated previously, it appears to me that throughout the book of Revelation blood is used as a judgment because humanity has rejected the most valuable blood of Jesus and has shed the blood of God's people. The Lord fulfilled the prayers of the saint under the altar of Incense in the fifth seal (Rev 6:9-11).

[506] Everything that the Father creates has life and can speak. The eagle in Revelation 8:13 speaks; the horns of the golden altar speak (Revelation 9:13); the trees clap their hands (Isaiah 55:12), the creation groans for deliverance (Romans 8), etc.

[507] This heat from the sun is probably literal and may also be spiritual affliction (compare Mark 4:5-6 w/Mark 4:16-17; Revelation 7:14-16).

[508] They apparently had the name of the beast (blasphemy) and the mark of the beast (blasphemy) and the number of the beast (mans' blasphemy).

10 And the fifth angel poured out his **bowl** upon the **throne** of the beast; and his kingdom was full of darkness; and they chewed their tongues for pain.

11 And blasphemed[509] the God of heaven,[510] because of their pains and their ulcers, and not **they-changed-mind**[511] out-of their **acts.**

12 And the sixth angel poured out his **bowl** upon the **mega** river Euphrates; and the water thereof was dried up,[512] that the way of the kings of the **rising sun** might be **internally-prepared.**

---

[509] Blasphemy is their nature. The name of the beast is blasphemy, and this proves that the beast and his kingdom walked in the name of the beast (blasphemy) and the mark of the beast (blasphemy) and the number of the beast (blasphemy).

[510] "God of heaven" is a phrase that Daniel 2:44 associates with God setting up His kingdom on earth during the time of the ten (10) toes (kings). These ten (10) kings are also discussed in Revelation 13, Revelation 17, and Daniel 7.

[511] One of the purposes of God's judgments is an attempt to get mankind to repent.

[512] This bowl dries up the holding place (Euphrates, fruitful; the Hebrew root word means to break forth, the gushing forth) of the four angels released by the 6th Trumpet; hence the 100,000,000 horsemen implicitly are now removed to make the way for the kings of the east. In other words, the four angels that were prepared and loosed only to kill were once again bound to allow the way for the kings of the east. It is also worthy to note that because this plague ceased, this may become a self-imposed deception of the deceived to fight against God since there is now no hindrance to the gathering of kings (leaders) and their followers against the Lord Jesus.

13 And **I-perceived** three unclean spirits[513] like frogs[514] out of the mouth of the dragon, and out of the mouth of the beast, and out of the mouth of the false prophet.[515]

14 For they are the spirits of devils, **making signs**[516] go forth to the kings of the whole **habitable-house**, to gather them to the battle of **that day, the mega,** of God **the** Almighty.

15 Be-perceiving, I-am-coming[517] as a thief. Blessed *is* he that watches, and **guard** his garments, lest he walk naked, and they **look-at**[518] his **disfigurement.**[519]

---

[513] The spirit of the false prophet is also called the spirit of the Antichrist (1 John 4:1-3); the spirit of the beast is also called the prince of Greece (Daniel 7:6 w/Daniel 10); the spirit of the dragon is the original serpent, the Devil and Satan (2 Corinthians 11:3-4).

[514] In the days of Jannes and Jambres, Moses multiplied frogs in Egypt as a judgment; and Jannes and Jambres of Egypt also did the same (multiply frogs). It was only Moses who could also destroy the frogs. It other words, the dragon, the beast, and the false prophet can only multiply uncleanness with frog demons; however, only Jesus can get rid of the frog demons.

[515] The false prophet's alias is "another beast" (Revelation 13:11).

[516] In 2 Thessalonians 2:9, it is stated that Satan will work all signs, wonders, and powers of falsehood to deceive (recruit) those who refuse the love of the Truth (Jesus).

[517] Proof that Jesus will not come as a thief before the beast with all its blasphemy comes on the scene. In fact, it was right in the middle of the three beast recruitment that Jesus said He would come as a thief, not before.

[518] The dragon, the beast and the false prophet will be able to see ("look at") those who have "shame" related to sexual immorality (see the next note below) in order to recruit them. In other words, they have the ability to discern nakedness that relates to degrading sexuality.

[519] The Greek word "disfigurement" is used in one other place in reference to homosexuality and lesbianism (Romans 1:27); the dragon, the beast and the false prophet will be recruiting those who are trapped in the shame of homosexuality and lesbianism. It is also necessary to note that legalism of same sex marriage, does not make it acceptable to God. It also appears that the beast will have no

16 And he gathered them together into a place called in the Hebrew tongue **Armageddon.**[520]

17 And the seventh angel poured out his **bowl** into the air;[521] and there came a **mega** voice out of the temple of heaven, from the throne, saying, **it-has-become.**[522]

18 And there were voices, and thunders, and lightnings; and there was a **mega** earthquake, such as was not since men were upon the earth, an earthquake **such-as-this,** so **mega.**

19 And the **mega** city[523] was divided into three parts,[524] and the cities of the nations' fell;[525] and **mega** Babylon came in

---

desire for women (Daniel 11:37). With that said, Jesus provided therapy to catamites who came to Him seeking healing.

[520] Most of the texts say "Armageddon" ("mountain-crowd" or "mountain of Megiddo"). With that said, there is no "mountain of Megiddo" in the natural. Therefore, it begs the question, is Armageddon a spiritual principle that points to a spiritual mountain? If Armageddon is to be considered as spiritual, then Armageddon may be a mountain of people (as seen in the word "crowd"). That is, the amount of people that will be recruited by the three beasts will be so many that it may be like a mountain of people that will consummate in their destruction in Revelation 19 by Jesus, the King of kings and Lord of lords.

[521] There is a prince of the authority of the air (Ephesians 2:1-2); sacrifice-wrath will be poured on the air judging the prince and preparing the air to be occupied by the saints in the coming of the Lord (1 Thessalonians 4:17). That is, righteous will be established (dwell) in the heavens (3 Peter 3:13).

[522] This may point to the time when Mystery Babylon's judgment is consummated.

[523] Is this city that will be divided due to the great earthquake, the Vatican City?

[524] Mystery Babylon will be divided into three parts. See also the next section, "Manifestations from our Lord Jesus Lord Jesus," subtitled, "Mystery Babylon Divided into Three."

[525] Cities of nations shall fall; and it appears that the saints will inherit them and will shepherd them with a rod of iron during the millennium rule (Psalms 2:9; Revelation 2:27; 12:5; Revelation 19:15).

remembrance before God, to give to her the cup of the wine of the **sacrifice-wrath of-the**[526] his **grasping-anger**.

20 And every island[527] fled away, and the mountains[528] were not found.[529]

21 And there fell upon men a **mega** hail[530] out of heaven, talent-like;[531] and men blasphemed[532] God because of the plague of the hail; for the plague thereof was **mega, vehemently-violent**.

---

[526] "Wrath" is genitive case (source) in the Greek text; hence, grasping-anger is the "source" of His "sacrifice-wrath."

[527] This can refer to literal islands. If in a negative sense, this can represent people isolated by the sea of humanity that will flee when this bowl of wrath is poured out.

[528] These mountains may also be spiritual mountains. John, the Baptist was sent to also affect (spiritual) mountains (Luke 3:5). John did not make any literal mountain low; therefore, Luke 3:5 was referring to spiritual mountains. Ezekiel 35 speaks of the "mountain of Seir." "Seir" is akin to the Hebrew word for "goat-demon." Hence, there is a spiritual mountain of demons. There are also the mountains of religion (Babylon (foreshadowing the false religion of Mystery Babylon) is called a burnt mountain and a destroying mountain in Jeremiah 51:25). The House of the Lord is also called "the mountain of the Lord's house" and God's mountain shall be established in the top of all other mountains (Isaiah 2:4). In other words, God's mountain house will overcome and conquer all other mountains, including, but not limited to the seven mountains of the beast in Revelation 17.

[529] The fact that mountains and islands can move to a place of not being found demonstrates the severity of the effect of the bowls; compare the dreadfulness of God's face from which the heaven and earth fled as fugitives, and no place was found for them (Revelation 20:11).

[530] God's reserves for the day of battle, trouble, and war (Job 38:22-23)

[531] "Talent-like" used in this verse is not by accident but is by God's design as every word of God is purposed. Therefore, is the "talent-like" related to the "goods" of Matthew 25:14-30? In other words, are the talents distributed by Jesus to His Church related to judgments to be executed as in Exodus 9:18-29?

[532] The fact that they blasphemed God is proof that these who blasphemed God had received the name of the beast on their foreheads (thoughts).

CHAPTER 17

1 And there came one of the seven angels[533] which had the seven bowls, and talked with me, saying to me, come here; I will show to you the judgment of the **mega female-prostitute**[534] that sits[535] upon many waters.[536]

2 With whom the kings of the earth have **prostituted**,[537] and the **dwellers** of the earth have been made drunk with the wine[538] of her **prostitution**.

---

[533] This "angel" is a fellow prophet and priest (prophet-priest), as we will see later in this commentary.

[534] The great prostitutes is symbolic of counterfeit religious systems of the world that existed from the days that the first murder was committed by Cain, since Revelation 18:24 indicated that she is responsible for "all" the bloodshed on the earth. She is the adulteress "in" the eyes of humanity (2 Pet 2:14, Zech. 5:6).

[535] She sits upon many waters, she sits upon the beast, she sits upon seven heads, she sits upon seven mountains, she sits upon people, multitudes, nations, and tongues, she sits upon the ephah. All these places she "sit"s are synonymous. (Revelation 17; Zechariah 5:5-11).

[536] "Many waters" is symbolic of the scarlet-colored beast (Revelation 17:3; "many waters" is also symbolic of seven mountains (continents are basically the top of mountains) (Revelation 17:9); some believe this points to the headquarters of the Roman Catholic Church that sits on seven hills; "many waters" is also symbolic of multitudes, nations (ethnics), kindred and tongues (literal or speech) (Revelation 17:15).

[537] "Porne" (translated as porno), from the root word "pernemi" to export for sale.

[538] Kinds of wine—natural wine, wine sex (prostitution sex or marriage sex is also as wine); there is also the anger wine, wine of self-rejection.

3 So he carried me away in the spirit into the wilderness; and **I-perceived** a woman sit upon a scarlet[539] colored beast,[540] full of names of blasphemy,[541] having seven heads and ten horns.

4 And the woman was arrayed in purple and scarlet color, and **gilded** with gold and precious stones and pearls,[542] having a golden cup[543] in her hand full of **stink** and **uncleansed** of her **prostitution of the earth**.

5 And upon her forehead[544] a name written,[545] **secret, Babylon,**[546] **the mega, the mother**[547] **of female-prostitutes**[548] **and stinks**[549] of the earth.

---

[539] Scarlet is a symbol of wealth (Lamentation 4:5, Daniel 5:16); scarlet is also a symbol for sins (Isaiah 1:18).

[540] Some believe that this represents religions that are State sponsored; however, not all religious undertaking that is State sponsored is negative. Ezra received some support from Medes and Persia during the reconstruction of Jerusalem.

[541] The same beast of Revelation 13; except here its described as being "full" or "swelled out" with blasphemy.

[542] Does this type of clothing remind you of the Catholic Church and all her daughters (orthodox religion)?

[543] Spiritual cup filled with the wine of uncleanness, abominations, and prostitutions.

[544] Babylon has a harlot's forehead; "she refuses to be ashamed" (Jeremiah 3:3).

[545] In the book of Revelation, there are three entities that write on the forehead, two of which are against God. The false prophet encourages the beast's name, mark, and number to be written in the forehead. Mystery Babylon also has her name written on her forehead. The proper thing to be written on the forehead is the name of God and the Lamb of God.

[546] The name "Babylon" is of Hebrew origin, and it is defined as confusion, mix, mingle, overflow with oil, anoint, feed (Strong's Old Testament #894, #1101, #1098); this points to the confusion that is in religions of the world, religions that do not accept Jesus as "the Christ," the Son of the living God. This is also religious systems that walk in "confused [pseudo] anointing." The Hebrew hieroglyphics for Babylon is "house-of-failure," "internal-failure, house-leading astray, internal leading astray."

6 And **I-perceived** the woman drunken with the blood[550] of the saints, and with the blood of the martyrs[551] of Jesus; and when **I-perceived** her, I **marveled** with mega **marvel**.

7 And the angel said to me, why did you marvel? I will tell you the **secret** of the woman, and of the beast that carries her, which has the seven heads and ten horns.

---

[547] Babylon mothered many religious systems that bear her name—"confusion" (contrast 1 Corinthians 14:33—"God is not of confusion ...").

[548] Some believe and teach that there is Mystery Babylon, the mother (headquarters) of a religious system, and there are her daughters (the many denominations or satellite locations) of that same system. Mystery Babylon's daughters may also consist of false religions such as: Hinduism, Buddhism, Voodoo, Idol worship, ancestral worship, Jehovah Witnesses, who believe that Jesus is only a prophet, and they oppose that Jesus is the Christ, the son of the living God; Islam also believes that Jesus is only a prophet; the Catholic Church preaches that people should pray to Mary in addition to emphasizing prayer to so called saints, none of which is biblical; Mormonism also has teachings that are not biblical. The Bible said that one of the definitions of "antichrist" is that which is "instead of Christ." Saying that Jesus is only a prophet is "instead of Christ;" teaching to pray to Mary and so-called canonized saints is "instead of Christ." Are you aware that the bishopric that was established in the Pentecostal denominations was sanctioned by a Pope who granted them permission after some preachers solicited him? Thus, even the Pentecostal denomination is also "mothered" by Babylon. Who is your mother, New Jerusalem (Galatians 4:26), above, or another entity invented by men and fallen angels?

[549] Some of the things that are considered abominations are: Idols, coveting of money, and adultery (Luke 16:13-17; Ezekiel 8, etc.). Abominations or stinks also applies to defilements through bitterness, sexually defiling dreams, idols, defilements from stained souls (Heb 12:15, Titus 1:15-16, Jude 1:8, Rom 2:22, John 18:28 w/Leviticus 22:4-6).

[550] Shedding blood is synonymous with getting drunk with blood. Imagine how drunk a nation is that allows bloodshed from abortion, murder, terrorism, etc.

[551] Blood of martyrs is the blood of those who were killed for Jesus; while the blood of the saints represents whose blood was shed but were not necessarily killed.

8 The beast that you saw was,[552] and is not;[553] and **is-intending to-be-ascending out-of** the **abyss**,[554] and go into perdition; and they that dwell on the earth shall **marvel**, whose names were not written in the Book of Life[555] from the foundation of the world, when they **look-at** the beast that was, and is not, and **shall-be-present**.[556]

9 And here the mind which has wisdom.[557] The seven heads are seven mountains,[558] on which the woman **is-sitting**.

---

[552] This beast existed before (the system of the beast previously existed, or he lived previously).

[553] This beast died and went to the abyss.

[554] The place where the dead abide (Romans 10:7); this beast ("first" king of the previous seven (7) will rise again to become the eighth (8th)); he "was, and is not, yet is"—is this the same spirit of Greece that governed with Alexander, the Great and that also influenced Alexander, the Great that will rise again? It seems so (see Daniel 8, Daniel 10).

[555] If your name is written in the Book of Life, you will not be deceived to marvel at the beast or worship the beast.

[556] Revelation 13:14 indicates the same concept and is referring to the same beast.

[557] Jesus is made unto us Wisdom and the Wisdom of God (1 Corinthians 1:24; 30); hence, only the Christian minds that hold Jesus (having the mind of Christ (1 Corinthians 2:16)) can fully understand the mystery of the beast and the great prostitute and therefore avoid their pitfalls.

[558] Most land masses are basically the tops of mountains which bottoms are under the ocean; hence these seven mountains may be a symbol of the seven continents, symbol of spiritual mountains (Luke 3:5 w/John 10:41); symbol of the high place of idolatry (Jeremiah 3:6, Isiah 57:7); symbol of kingdoms (Daniel 2, Isaiah 2)

10 And there are seven kings; five are fallen, and one is,[559] the other[560] is not yet come; and **whenever** he comes, he must **remain puny**.

11 And the beast that was,[561] and is not,[562] even he is the eighth, and is **out-of**[563] the seven, and goes into perdition.

12 And the ten horns which **you-perceived** are ten kings,[564] which have received no kingdom as yet;[565] but receive **authority** as kings **first**[566] hour with the beast.

---

[559] Since a beast with its sixth (6th) head existed in the days of John, the number of the beast, the mark of the beast and beast worship also existed in John's days as it does in every age from Daniel until Jesus eventually eradicates them. For further understanding, the reader may also refer to my Book titled, *The Numbers of God,* and the chapter titled "6."

[560] This is the seventh (7th) head; seven is the number of rest; therefore, a season of relative "rest" for the saints from persecution by the beast system

[561] This means that this beast lived and/or ruled once before.

[562] This beast (a king and his kingdom) died and will yet live.

[563] He is "out-of the seven" because he once lived as the "first" head (see Revelation 13:3 w/Revelation 13:14).

[564] According to Daniel 7, these will revive out of the Roman Empire (present day Europe).

[565] The reason they are not crowned as in Revelation 13 is because they have received no kingdom as of yet. This may mean that the events of Revelation 13 may take place after Revelation 17. It is also worthy to note that none of the seven heads of the beast were crowned in revelation 13 or Revelation 17. The reason is that Satan wears the seven crowns in Revelation 12, and therefore the dragon is the ruling spirit over these seven heads/kings. This truth is seen in Daniel 10 where there is an invisible prince that rules over Greece and invisible princes that rule over Medes and Persia.

[566] This is probably the first hour (~42 years) of the millennium to come; per 2 Peter 3:8, one (1) day with the Lord is as a thousand (1,000) years; hence, (1000 years/24 hours=41.66 years/hours (~42 years per hour). John 2:18 speaks of a "last hour" (~42 years) of the age he lived in (depicted by his definition of antichrists); therefore, there must be a "first hour" of the next age. The beast's resurrected rule appears to be the first hour of the age to come. Or the first hour

13 These have **first opinion**,[567] and shall **give-throughout** their **authority** and **power** to the beast.[568]

14 These shall make war with the Lamb,[569] and the Lamb shall overcome them;[570] for he is Lord of lords, and King of kings; and they that are with him called, and chosen, and **believing**.

15 And he says to me, the waters which **you-perceived**, where the **female-prostitute is-sitting**,[571] are peoples, and multitudes, and nations, and tongues.

---

may be symbolic of one half of a full prophetic week of years (360/24=15 years/hour; 15 years=1 hour; hence ½ hour=7.5 years or 7 years depending on the true Hebrew calendar year based on 7 days/week). For further development, see my book titled: *The Last Hour, The First Hour, the 42ⁿᵈ Generation.*

[567] Read in context of Revelation 17:16-17. The first opinion of the ten horns (ten kings) appears to be the plan (opinion) to burn Mystery Babylon with fire, eat her flesh (war against her) and make her naked (take all her clothing and riches).

[568] The leopard beast or the spirit of Greece; Gabriel in Daniel 8 called "the rough goat" (lit., goat-demon) the king of Greece and also called the "great horn" the king of Greece. The "great horn" was broken off (Alexander the great died); however, the goat-demon (the spirit of Greece) continued on, and four other horns came up out of the goat-demon after Alexander died and eventually "a little horn **out of the 'first'** of them" also grew out of the same goat-demon. The "first of them" was "the great horn," Alexander, the great that is also alluded with respect to death by sword and "yet did live" in Revelation 13: 2-3a w/Revelation 13:12 w/Revelation 17:8-11.

[569] This can be understood as making war with Jesus' saints; and thus, making war with the Lamb (Acts 9:4-5 w/Acts 9:1-5).

[570] Jesus always wins! I admonish you to stay on the winning team if you already follow the Lord Jesus; and if you are not a believer into Jesus, join His winning team.

[571] This sitting of her on peoples, multitudes, nations, and tongues must be seen in the context of pollution (compare Jeremiah 3:1).

16 And the ten horns which you saw **and** the beast; these shall hate the **female-prostitute**,[572] and shall make her desolate and naked, and shall eat her flesh,[573] and burn her with fire.

17 For God **give into** their hearts to **do the opinion of him**,[574] and to **do first**[575] **opinion**, and give their kingdom to the beast, until the **declarations**[576] of God shall be **finished**.[577]

18 And the woman which **you-perceived is the city**,[578] the mega, **having a kingdom**[579] over the kings of the earth.

---

[572] If the ten horns represent the kingdoms (ten kingdoms of a future EU (spirit of Greece), or the world divided into ten domains), these kings will hate the harlot, burn her, and eat her flesh (make war against her), which many believe is the Catholic Church and her various offspring, including, but not limited to, all of her adultery with idols/images and her spiritual fornication (selling religion) with the kings of the earth. I must also note that Islam, Buddhism, etc. also influence kings.

[573] "Eat her flesh" is a metaphor for the beast "warring" against her. A Hebrew word for translated as "war" is also translated "to eat." Eating her flesh also represents the beast destroying all who are joined to her "flesh" (1 Cor 6:15-16)

[574] God has an "opinion" of the prostitute and the beast, and His opinion trumps any other purposes.

[575] They will give their kingdom to the beast in order to complete the opinion of God, which is to judge the great prostitute.

[576] Jesus said that every (all) words of God shall be fulfilled.

[577] Believe it or not, the reign of the beast and the ten horns is to fulfill God's Word. "And the king shall do according to his will; and he shall exalt himself, and magnify himself above every god, and shall speak marvelous things against the God of gods and shall prosper until the indignation be accomplished; for that that is determined shall be done" (Daniel 11:36, KJV).

[578] The woman prostitute (Babylon) is also called a city.

[579] It does appear that most false religions of the world rule (have a kingdom) over kings (leaders). Some believe, this is the Catholic system, the Vatican City that rules over nations. I must also note that Islam, Buddhism, etc. also rules over nations and influence kings.

CHAPTER 18

1 And after these things I saw another angel come down from heaven, having **mega authority**;[580] and the earth was **illuminated out-of** his glory.[581]

2 And he cried[582] with a **mega** voice, saying, Babylon the **mega** is fallen, is fallen, and is become the **dwelling**[583] of

---

[580] In order to have great authority, one must be "under authority," not "in" authority. There is only one person **"in"** authority and that is God, the Father, Jesus, and the Holy Spirit (Matthew 8:7-10).

[581] This principle was first spoken of concerning the Lord Jesus in Ezekiel 43:2. Hence, this speaks of Jesus who will illuminate the entire earth with His glory. There will also arise in the earth messengers of the gospel who through the Spirit will receive the revelation of their glory (1 Corinthians 2:7 w/1 Corinthians 2:10-11; John 2:11 w/John 2:1-11). Their glory will be with such authority the earth will be illuminated with their glory. Saying it another way, this angel manifesting "his glory" can represent, messengers of our Lord Jesus who have heard things in the Spirit to "their" glory. Jesus manifested (shined) "his" glory (John 2:11). Paul said we can also manifest some spiritual things to "our" glory (1 Corinthians 2:7). Jesus wants to bring "many sons 'into' glory" (Hebrews 2:10).

[582] Sometimes the gospel must be heard through a "cry" that may be forceful and harassing; Job indicated that "right words" are "forcible" or "harassing" (Job 6:25, KJV).

[583] "The Spirit speaks 'explicitly' that in the later times some shall depart from the faith 'becoming holding-ones' of seducing spirits and doctrines of 'demons'" (1 Timothy 4:1). Impure religions and defiled religions are places of demons, spirits, and hateful birds. Jesus emphasized relationship with the Father and the Son (Jesus Christ) not religion of angels (ceremonial observances, formal public rituals). God's living Temple made up of His people is for God's permanent habitation with His Spirit (Eph 2:19-22); however, apostate religions are a habitation of demons, unclean spirits, beasts, and unclean birds (Rev 18:1-3).

demons,[584] and the **guard-place**[585] of every unclean spirit,[586] and a **guard-place** of every unclean and hateful bird.[587]

3 For all nations have drunk of the wine of the **sacrifice-wrath** of her **prostitution**,[588] and the kings of the earth have **prostituted** with her, and the merchants of the earth are waxed rich through the **power** of her **straining**.[589]

4 And I heard another voice from heaven, saying, come out of her,[590] my people, that you be not partakers of her sins,[591] and that you receive not of her plagues.

---

[584] Doctrines of demons are the source for Mystery Babylon (the religious systems of the world)—1 Timothy 4:1, Colossians 2:18, James 3:15 w/James 3:13-15.

[585] Spurious religious systems that will guard their demons (they will not allow the truth of God to dispel them).

[586] Unclean spirits here may show spirits that cry out against Jesus, etc. (Luke 4:32-34).

[587] Birds in a cage represent "fraud" in false religion (Jeremiah 5:27).

[588] Prostitution carries anger that can lead to death and murder. It's well documented that some serial killers were heavy into to porno.

[589] There are many who strain against God, in order not to do His will; and there is a "power" behind that straining that brings deceptive riches.

[590] In the Old Testament God allowed Israel to be under the captivity of natural Babylon for preservation; the same is true for mystery Babylon (looking only at orthodox religion). Though used by God as a preservation, there will come a time when Jesus' true followers must leave the religious systems as God is about to "plague" that system for her corruption.

[591] Daniel 1:8-17 where Daniel and his friends refuse to "redeem." Or "marry" the defilements related to the "dainties" and "wine" of Babylon, though they were in captivity there.

5 For her sins have reached to heaven,[592] and God has remembered her iniquities.[593]

6 Reward her even as she rewarded, and double to her double[594] according to her works. In the cup[595] which she has filled[596] fill to her double.

7 How much she has glorified herself,[597] and lived **straining,** so much torment and sorrow give her; for she says in her

---

[592] Something similar happened with Sodom and Gomorrah, the "cry" of their sin "came unto [the Lord"]; in other words, the sin of Sodom and Gomorrah reached heaven where the Lord dwells (Genesis 18:20-21).

[593] In Hebrews 10:17, the Bible said that God does **not** remember our sins once we accept the sacrifice of Jesus Christ; therefore, for Mystery Babylon's iniquities to be remembered, she must **not** have really accepted the blood and sacrifice of Jesus (compare Revelation 2:21 w/Revelation 9:21); or Mystery Babylon fulfilled Ezekiel 18:24.

[594] Instead of receiving a double portion of blessings, she will receive a double portion of plagues according to her polluted work.

[595] We are admonished to drink from the proper cup of the Lord Jesus, not other cups (1 Corinthians 10:21). We are admonished not to drink from the cup of demons (1 Corinthians 10:21); and we are not to drink of the cup of Mystery Babylon (Revelation 17:4).

[596] The same cup that had was filled with her prostitution and abominations (including manmade images of so called saints); will be filled again with double plagues.

[597] According to John 7:18, this means that she speaks of herself, from herself and about herself (compare Proverbs 25:27). Remember this is also a sin of Satan (John 8:44).

heart, I sit a queen,[598] and am no widow,[599] and shall see no sorrow.[600]

8 Therefore shall her plagues **arrive** in **first** day, death, and mourning, and famine;[601] and she shall be utterly burned with fire; for **forcible**[602] the Lord God who **has judged** her.

9 And the kings of the earth, **prostitute with her** and lived **straining** with her, shall bewail her, and lament for her, when they shall see the smoke of her burning.

10 Standing afar off for the fear of her torment, saying, **woe, woe**, that **mega** city Babylon, that **forcible** city! For in **first**[603] hour is your judgment come.

11 And the merchants of the earth shall weep and mourn over her; for no man buys their merchandise any more.

12 The merchandise of gold, and silver, and precious stones, and of pearls, and fine linen, and purple, and silk, and scarlet, and all **fragrant**[604] wood, and all manner vessels of ivory, and

---

[598] Compare the use of the word "queen" in Jeremiah 7:18; 44:18-25 in reference to incense (prayers) and offerings (relics?), etc.

[599] This implies that she refuses to believe that she was without a husband. We also read in Revelation 18:23 that in her was "the voice of the bridegroom" (Jesus); and just because she claims to have the voice of the bridegroom, does not mean that she is married to Jesus, in truth.

[600] This was presumptuous of her because God did not share this opinion of her as seen in the next verse, Revelation 18:8, her "mourning" came in the first hour.

[601] Or hunger

[602] God was forceful against her because she is too forceful (Revelation 18:10).

[603] 1 John 2:18 speaks of a "last hour" of his age (depicted by antichrists); therefore, there must be a "first hour" of the next age. Will mystery Babylon be judged in the first hour of the age to come? For further development, see my book titled: *The Last Hour, The First Hour, The 42nd Generation.*

[604] Greek: Thuinon (root for this word means to breathe hard)-a fragrant tree

all manner vessels of most precious wood, and of brass, and iron, and marble,

13 And cinnamon, and odors, and ointments, and frankincense, and wine, and oil, and fine flour, and wheat, and **domestic-animals**, and sheep, and horses, and chariots, and **bodies**,[605] and souls[606] of men.

14 And the fruits that your soul lusted after are departed from you and all things which were **fat** and **radiant** are departed from you, and you shall **not-still** find them.

15 The merchants of these things, which were made rich by her, shall stand afar off for the fear of her torment, **sobbing** and wailing,

16 And saying, **woe, woe**, that **mega** city, that was clothed[607] in fine linen,[608] and purple,[609] and scarlet,[610] and **gilded** with gold,[611] and precious stones,[612] and pearls![613]

---

[605] "Bodies" includes, but not limited to aborted body parts of babies, adults selling surgically removed body parts, human trafficking, etc.

[606] According to Leviticus 17:11: "the 'soul' of the flesh is in the blood."

[607] Note: All her clothing may point to outward ornaments as opposed to the Lamb's wife whose clothing was spiritual (contrast Revelation 12:1).

[608] This "fine linen" may be literal linen, or it may point to the pseudo righteous acts of mystery Babylon, but her righteous acts are not "white and clean" as the Lamb's wife's (the Church) fine linen was clean and white in Revelation 19:8.

[609] A royal color and points to her reigning over the kings of the earth through her prostitution, or it may be literal purple.

[610] Points to the blood of Jesus that she and her daughters use erroneously, or it could be literal scarlet clothing, or it could represent the blood of humans that she killed (Revelation 17:6; 18:24); or it could represent wealth (Lamentation 4:5, Daniel 5:16); sins (Isaiah 1:18).

[611] False glory or literal gold

[612] False gifts (Proverbs 17:8) or literal precious stones

[613] A false claim of being bought by Jesus, or they are literal pearls

17 For in **first** hour[614] **so-much** riches are come to nothing. And every **navigator**,[615] and all the company **of** ships,[616] and sailors, and as many as trade by sea,[617] stood afar off,

18 And cried when they saw the smoke of her burning, saying, what like to this **mega** city!

19 And they cast dust on their heads, and cried, weeping, and wailing, saying, **woe, woe,** that **mega** city, wherein were made rich[618] all that had **floaters** in the sea by reason of her **expensiveness**![619] For in **first** hour is she made desolate!

20 Rejoice over her, the heaven, **and the saints, and the** apostles and **the** prophets;[620] for God has **judged your**[621] **judgment out-of** her.

---

[614] First 42 years of a millennium; per 2 Peter 3:8, one (1) day with the Lord is as a thousand (1,000) years; hence, (1000 years/24 hours=41.66 Years (~42 years).

[615] Or pilot; compare "government" (KJV) in 1 Corinthians 12:28.

[616] "Ships" may also point to the execution of ministry (positive or negative). Jesus ministered from ships (Matthew 13:2, Mark 1:16-17); and Paul was conveyed via a ship to preach at Rome (Acts 27-Acys 28).

[617] Literal sea, and it can also point to the sea of humanity

[618] The love of money seems to make men cry more than anything else. They were more concerned about their riches rather than repenting.

[619] "Her expensiveness" may point to religious entities and religious people who spend more money on expensive worldly things (manmade sanctuaries (Hebrews 9:1); abnormal use of the fashion of the world (1 Corinthians 7:31); conspicuous consumption (1 John 2:16); etc.

[620] Apostles and prophets still exist today as they did in the early days of Christianity. Thus, God specifically mentions their requested judgment on her; and this "judgment" is one of the functions of the apostles and prophets (see below). Apostles and prophets are "foundation" ministries (Ephesians 2:19-22).

[621] Apostles and prophets are authorized to judge, direct, command and predict.

21 And a **forcible** angel took up a stone like a **mega** millstone, and cast into the sea, saying, thus with violence[622] shall that **mega** city Babylon be thrown down, and shall **not-still** be found.

22 And the voice of harpers,[623] and musicians, and of pipers, and trumpeters,[624] shall be heard no more at all in you; and no craftsman,[625] of whatsoever craft,[626] shall be found any more in you; and the sound of a millstone shall be heard no more at all in you;

23 And the light of a candle[627] shall shine no more at all in you; and the voice of the bridegroom[628] and of the bride[629] shall be heard no more at all in you; for your merchants were the **mega** men of the earth; for by your **drugs** were all nations **strayed**.

---

[622] Babylon being thrown down is compared to a millstone being cast into the sea; hence she must have offended "one of these little ones"—those who not only believe in Jesus, but they were also "converted" through Jesus (Matthew 18:6).

[623] Remember that Babylon means confusion; therefore, these harpers (worshippers) are confused worshippers. They may be compared to Jesus's statement to the Samaritan woman, "[They] worship what [they] do not know" (John 4:22). That is, they may think they are worshipping God because of a particular edifice; but they are void of true worship (John 4:21-24).

[624] "Confused" prophets (since they are Babylonians prophets)

[625] "Technicians," architects, and craftsmen

[626] This craft includes technology that is used improperly.

[627] This is light that is really not the light of God (Matthew 6:21-24)

[628] This is the part of Mystery Babylon's system that cites Jesus (the bridegroom) as her husband; yet it's a false claim due to her prostitution with idols, invented gods, worldly images, praying to dead so called saints and prophets, etc. that confuses people.

[629] The false claim of being the bride of Jesus; yet is serving various idolatrous doctrines that confuses the weak minds. This understanding can narrow "mystery Babylon" down to any prostitute entity (apostate church) who claim to be part of the bride of Christ.

24 And in her was found the blood of prophets, and of saints, and of all[630] that were slain upon the earth.

CHAPTER 19

1 And after these things I heard **something like** a **mega** voice of much people in heaven, saying, alleluia, salvation, and glory, and honor, and power, to the Lord our God.

2 For true and righteous his judgments; for he has judged the **mega female-prostitute,** which did **rot**[631] the earth **in** her **prostitution,**[632] and has avenged the blood of his servants at her hand.

3 And again they said, alleluia; and her smoke **is-ascending into the ages of ages.**

4 And the twenty-four elders and the four **living-things** fell down and worshipped God that **is-sitting** on the throne, saying, amen; alleluia.

---

[630] Hence Mystery Babylon is all the counterfeit religious systems of the world that have shed the blood from the days of Abel and Cain in Genesis 4. In other words, mystery Babylon has been around since the beginning since she is also secretly responsible for Abel's bloodshed ("in her was found the blood ... of all the were slain on the earth"); see also Luke 11:47-51 where bloodshed can cause judgment of the parents and the children of those who shed blood.

[631] This is included in the judgment executed by the 7th angel in the 7th trumpet (Revelation 11:15-18).

[632] Prostitution (spiritual or natural prostitution) causes things to rot (or to be corrupted). This is probably one of the reasons prostitutes (male and female) and/or pervasive sexual immorality carries diseases that cause rotting. God said that a woman who has more than one husband is polluted (Jeremiah 3:1); however, having more than one husbands does not necessarily disqualify a woman from Jesus' salvation (John 4:1-42). This apostate woman corrupted the earth with her abominable idols, and prostitution with the unbelieving rulers in the earth

5 And a voice came out of the throne,[633] saying, praise our God, all you his servants, and you that fear him, both small and **mega**.

6 And I heard as it were the voice of a **much** multitude, and as the voice of **much water** and as the voice of **forcible** thunders, saying, alleluia, for the Lord God omnipotent reigns.

7 Let us be glad and rejoice and give honor to him; for the marriage of the Lamb is come and his wife[634] has made herself **internally-prepared**.[635]

8 And to her was granted that she should be arrayed in fine linen, clean and white; for the fine linen is the **righteousness-acts** of saints.

9 And he says to me, write: Blessed **the-ones** which are called to the marriage **dinner** of the Lamb. And he says to me, these are the true sayings of God.

10 And I fell at his feet to worship him. And he said to me, **stare** you not, I am your fellow servant, and of your brethren[636] that have the testimony of Jesus, worship God; for the testimony of Jesus is the spirit **'of-the'** prophecy.[637]

---

[633] The Throne of God also speaks. Everything that God creates has life and speaks. Jesus said, even the stones have the ability to cry out (Luke 19:40).

[634] The "great mystery" of the Church being Jesus' wife and bride (Ephesians 5:22-32); and she is also known as New Jerusalem (Revelation 21:9-10).

[635] Ephesians 5:27

[636] This angel is a brother (a human) of John and a fellow servant (a human); and he is also called a prophet (a human) in Revelation 22:8-9 and they functions as priests (Revelation 15:7-8).

[637] "The prophecy" is the witness (testimony) of Jesus. This is the same prophecy that the two witnesses preached. The two witnesses preached Jesus (Revelation 11:7)!

11 And **I-perceived** heaven opened and behold a white horse; and he **sitting** upon him called **Believing** and True, and in righteousness he doth judge and make war.

12 His eyes as a flame of fire, and on his head many crowns; and he has names written and a name written, that no man knew, **if not him**.

13 And he **was-clothed** with vesture dipped in blood;[638] and his name is called The Word of God.

14 And the armies in heaven followed him upon white horses, clothed in **pure white linen.**

15 And out of his mouth goes a sharp **two-edged** sword,[639] that with it he should smite the nations; and he shall **shepherd** them with a rod of iron;[640] and he[641] treads the winepress of the **sacrifice-wrath and grasping-anger** of Almighty God.

---

[638] Was his vesture dipped in the blood of the wickedness that was pressed out in the winepress of His wrath? See Isaiah 63:2-3 w/Joel 3:12-14 w/Revelation 14:29-20.

[639] This how Jesus shall consume the man of sin by "the sword of the Spirit, which is the Word of God;" that is, "the Spirit of His mouth" (Ephesians 6:17; 2 Thessalonians 2:8).

[640] This phrase foremost was used for Jesus in Revelation 19:15. However, most of what applies to Jesus, the pattern Son, also applies to God's many sons (Revelation 12:5; 2:23); and according to Psalms 2:7-9, Revelation 2:23 is a "sonship" principle. David gathered the courage to declare what God said of him and the Messiah, "I will declare the decree: the LORD has said unto me, you are my Son; this day have I begotten you. 8Ask of me, and I shall give you the heathen for your inheritance, and the uttermost parts of the earth for your possession. 9You shall break them with a rod of iron; you shall break them in pieces like a potter's vessel."

[641] Isaiah 63:2-3 said that God "alone" will tread the winepress and that His garment may be made red by the blood of wickedness that will be pressed out of the un-persuadable. See the notes for Revelation 14:19-20 for further development.

16 And he has on vesture and on his thigh a name written, King of kings,[642] and Lord of lords.[643]

17 And I saw **one**[644] angel standing in the sun; and he cried with a **mega** voice, saying to all the fowls that fly in **mid-heaven**,[645] come and gather yourselves together to the **mega supper of the God.**

18 That you may eat the flesh of kings, and the flesh of captains, and the flesh of **forcible** men, and the flesh of horses, and of them that sit on them, and the flesh of all, free and slaves, both small and **mega**.

19 And I saw the beast, and the kings of the earth, and their armies, gathered together[646] to make war against him that sat on the horse, and against his army.

20 And the beast was taken,[647] and with him the false prophet[648] that wrought signs before him, with which he deceived them that had received the **engraving** of the beast,

---

[642] This phrase, King of kings and Lord of lords, is used by Paul relative to the times and seasons of Jesus' physical "appearing," again, to show that He is the only dynasty (1 Timothy 6:14-15). This "appearing" is also defined as the "brightness (appearing) of His coming" in 2 Thessalonians 2:8.

[643] Elders of the Church of Jesus are also called "lords" (Revelation 7:14).

[644] Is this the voice of the archangel of 1 Thessalonians 4:16 which is to occur during Jesus' coming?

[645] These are birds like eagles, falcons, vultures, etc. (birds that can soar in the heights of mid-heaven with keen eyesight).

[646] This gathering is a result of the three unclean spirits that did false signs for the express purpose of gathering an army against the Lamb (Revelation 16:13-16).

[647] "Taken" is also defined as arrested, pressed by hoofs; the fact that the beast and the false prophet were pressed by hoofs may imply that the Lord and His armies "descended" to the earth during this battle.

[648] An alias for the second beast called "another beast" in Revelation 13:11

and them that worshipped his image. These both were cast alive into a lake of fire burning with **God-sulfur-lightning.**

21 And the **remaining-ones** were slain with the sword[649] which proceeded out of his mouth[650] of him **sitting** upon the horse; and all the fowls were filled with their flesh.

CHAPTER 20

1 And **I-perceived** an angel come down from heaven, having the key of the bottomless pit and a **mega** chain in his hand.

2 And he **use-vigor**[651] on the dragon, that **original** serpent, which is the Devil, and Satan, and bound[652] him a thousand years.[653]

3 And cast him into the **abyss,**[654] and **lock him,** and **seal up-above** him, that he should not still **stray** the nations, **until the**

---

[649] The sword of the Spirit, the Word of God (Ephesians 6:18, John 6:63)

[650] The spirit of His mouth (2 Thessalonians 2:8, John 6:63)

[651] It appears to me that this angel had to "use strength" to bind the Dragon because the Devil does not want to be bound in "the abyss" to meet the angel of the abyss (Abaddon) and his tormenting locust-scorpions for 1,000 years (Revelation 9:1-11).

[652] The angel could bind Satan because Jesus already weakened Satan according to Luke 11:21-22 and Revelation 12:8.

[653] Jesus will bind Satan for 1, 000 years, in order to rid the earth of all his deceptive influence for 1,000 years. At the end of the 1,000 years, after being taught by Jesus and His Church, some will yet follow Satan again showing that some men simply choose to follow evil in spite of the opportunity to be taught for 1,000 years without the deceptive influence of the Devil.

[654] There are other "king angels" like Abaddon in the abyss, whose locust-scorpions are tormentors. Remember demons and/or fallen angels don't like to be sent to the abyss (Luke 8:31).This is proven out again in Revelation 20:1-3 when an angel had to use strength to bind Satan in order to cast him into the abyss. Angels must be afraid of King Abaddon or Apollyon, the angel of the abyss (Revelation 9:11).

thousand years **finished**; and after these he must be loosed a **small time**.

4 And I saw thrones, and they **seated** upon them, and judgment was given to them; and the souls[655] of them that were **chopped off with an ax**[656] through the witness of Jesus, and through the Word of God, and **any-who** had not worshipped the beast, neither his image, neither had **taken the engraving** on their foreheads, or on their hands; and they lived and **kings** with Christ **'the'** thousand years.

5 But the rest[657] of the dead lived not again until the thousand years were finished. This is the first resurrection.[658]

---

[655] "The souls of them that were beheaded" also points to spiritual beheading through sufferings. Psalms 105:18 says of Joseph that "he was laid in iron." The Hebrew reads: "his soul came into 'ax-head.'" "Iron" is translated as ax head in 2 Kings 6:5. Hence, the soul being beheaded with an ax is related to suffering, not only literal death. Joseph experienced the ax-head of being hated by his brothers, the ax-head of slavery, the ax-head of being lied on, and the ax-head of two years in prison because he refused to commit adultery.

[656] For more detailed understanding, please refer to my book, titled, *Jesus' Resurrection, Our Inheritance.*

[657] No more resurrection until Revelation 20:12

[658] This applies to the resurrection of the just (Luke 14:14). The first resurrection is during the coming of the Lord Jesus according to the promise of God Paul stated in 1 Thess 4:13-18, "the dead in Christ will rise first." This first resurrection occurs during the "days of the 7th Trumpet also called the "last Trumpet" (Rev 11:15-19, 1 Cor 15:50-54).

6 Blessed[659] and holy he that has **course**[660] in the first resurrection;[661] on such the second death[662] has no **authority,**

---

[659] Jesus said those who partake in the resurrection of the just will also be "blessed." Thus, it appears to me that that resurrection of the just and the first resurrection is one and the same resurrection. There is also a **"better resurrection"** (Hebrews 11:35).

[660] There appears to be at least two (2) courses in the first resurrection— "the first-fruit Christ" (which is different from Jesus, the firstfruit) and "the dead in Christ shall rise first" in His coming). Ezekiel 45 and Ezekiel 48 also discuss two courses in dividing the inheritance for the priesthood—the first-fruit of the first-fruit and then the first-fruit, itself. This inheritance and distribution of the land is linked to the resurrection as seen in the word "oblation." The "oblation" (KJV) in Ezekiel 45 is defined from the Hebrew word as "heave offering" or a "rise" (offering). The root word for "heave offering" is "ruwm" (or RWM) and it is defined as "to rise," "to raise up," "lift up," etcetera. In Ezekiel 48:10, it called the **"holy 'rise';"** and in Ezekiel 48:14, it is called the "firstfruits of the land," which I believe is linked to the "blessed and **holy** is he who has part in the **first resurrection**." Thus, the distribution and inheritance of the land (the land of our bodies being glorified with different degrees of glory (intensity) depending on the **"seed"** (1 Corinthians 15:38) is linked to the first resurrection. In Ezekiel 48:12, Septuagint (LXX)), he distinguished between the inheritance of the first-fruit of the firstfruit being given to the sons of Zadok (righteous ones) that remained faithful to God (see Ezekiel 44, and Ezekiel 48:13 in the Septuagint (LXX) and KJV. The Levites (joined), who previously went astray, according to Ezekiel 44, received the rest of the first-fruit inheritance (the rest of the "oblation" or "rise"). Ezekiel also indicated that during the first resurrection the sons of Zadok would live closer to God as opposed to the Levites who went astray. That is, the Father did forgive the Levites for straying and allowed them to partake in the first resurrection (the oblation or "rise"); however, He also rewarded the sons of Zadok by allowing them to inherit (tenant) the first-fruit of the first-fruit of the land (the glory of resurrection that is different from the glory of the Levites (1 Corinthians 15:41-42); and the sons of Zadok were also rewarded to live closer to the sanctuary, the dwelling place of God. Note: Zadok point to **Jesus** our "King Zadok" (Melchizedek—King of Righteousness) and the sons of Zadok points to the many sons of Jesus who presses into the inheritance of the "firstborns." The Levites can point to the priesthood of believers, the Church that belongs to Jesus who will indeed be glorified with different degree of glory. Again, please read 1 Corinthians 15, Ezekiel 45 and 48 in the Septuagint (LXX), the same translation Jesus and the early apostles used.

152

but they shall be priests[663] of God and of Christ and **shall-be-kings**[664] with him[665] a thousand years.

7 And when the thousand years are **finished**, Satan shall be loosed out of his prison.[666]

---

[661] The first resurrection is during the coming of the Lord Jesus according to the promise of God Paul stated in 1 Thess 4:13-18, "the dead in Christ will rise first." This first resurrection occurs during the "days of the 7th Trumpet also called the "last Trumpet" (Rev 11:15-19, 1 Cor 15:50-54).

[662] The second death is the lake of fire (Rev 20:14). Those in Christ who rise first will not have to worry about the lake of fire, a place originally created for the Devil and his angels (Matt 25:41).

[663] Please refer to my notes directly above concerning the reward of the royal priesthood of Jesus. One of the functions of being a priest of God during the millennium is the "ministering" (lit., priest-work) of the gospel of God (see Romans 15:16). The Church must remember that she is a royal priesthood of Jesus' Melchizedek order; and if that is understood, the book of Revelation is filled with the function of Jesus our Great-High Priest and His priests administering the priesthood, seen in pictures or signs like "the temple of God" the golden altar, the seven lampstands, priests in their linen garments with the belts, the Ark of the Covenant, God's Throne, the Mercyseat, and so on.

[664] Compare 1 Corinthians 4:8

[665] Does this phrase "with him" have the same implication as Revelation 3:21? This phrase "with Him" is also used in Revelation 3:21 and appears to have the same implication. Studying the Tabernacle built by Moses, we can understand that reigning with Him, may mean reigning with Him right here on earth (the Ark was placed on the earth when the Tabernacle was erected), as it also implies that we will reign with Him in heaven (the last place the Ark was seen). That is, the resurrected saints will have the same ability as Jesus, the ability to migrate between heaven and earth.

[666] Humanity live a thousand years without the tempter being loosed. He will be loosed again to test humanity as the first Adam was tested, and as the last Adam (Jesus) was tested, and as the Church was tested before the millennium.

8 And shall go out to **stray**[667] the nations which are in the four quarters of the earth, Gog, and Magog,[668] to gather them together to battle; the number of whom as the sand of the sea.

9 And they went up on the breadth of the earth, and compassed the camp of the saints about, and the beloved city; and fire came down from God out of heaven and devoured them.

10 And the devil that **strayed** them was cast into the lake of fire and **God-sulfur-lighting**, where **also** the beast and the false prophet, and shall be tormented day and night **into the ages of the ages**.

11 And **I-perceived** a mega white throne, and him that sat on it, from whose face the earth and the heaven fled away;[669] and there was found no place for them.

12 And **I-perceived** the dead, small and **mega**, stand before **the throne**; and the books were opened; and another book was opened, which is of life; and the dead were judged out of

---

[667] This ability of Satan to stray the nations and as indicated in verses that followed this verse show that after God locked Satan up for 1,000 years and purged Satan's influence for the same 1,000 years; humanity still chose to follow Satan, hence their judgments. This also shows that some humans, in general, do what they do against God because they allow themselves to be deceived, strayed, by Satan.

[668] The times and season of the manifestation of Gog (Satan) and Magog (the people who follow Satan) is placed after the millennium; not before the millennium, as some eschatology teachers proclaim. It is clear from this reference in Revelation 20:8 that Ezekiel 38 and Ezekiel 39 will have its fulfillment after the millennium. Ezekiel 38:8 said, "After many days you [Gog] shall be visited; in the latter years you shall come into the land brought back from the sword gathered out of many people ...." This sounds similar to what was said of Satan in Revelation 20:7, "And when the thousand years are expired, Satan shall be loosed out of prison;" and it was after this that Gog (Satan) and Magog (the people of the land that follow Satan) were mentioned.

[669] It will be so fearful to see Jesus on His Throne that the earth and the heavens will run from Him with no place found for them.

154

those things which were written in the books,[670] according to their **acts**.

13 And the sea gave up the dead which were in **her**; and Death[671] and Hell[672] **gave** up the dead which were in them;[673] and they were judged **each** according to their acts.

14 And Death and Hell were cast into the lake of fire. This is the second death, **the lake of fire.**

15 And **if-any**[674] was not found written in the Book of Life was cast into the lake of fire.[675]

---

[670] There is the book of Jasher (straight, right) (Joshua 10:13, 2 Samuel 1:18), the book of Remembrance for those who feared the Lord and thought upon His name (Malachi 3:16); the book of wars (Numbers 21:14); have you fought in any spiritual warfare? There is the book of the Law (Nehemiah 8:8); the book of Psalms (Acts 1:20); etc.

[671] It seems to me that one of the purposes of Death was to produce life (1 Corinthians 15:36). However, rather than producing life with regards to humans, the "firstborn of death" was fear of "hunger" or the calamity of death-famine that "holds" humans in the "king of Terror" (Death) (Job 18:12-14). However, Jesus overcame death-hunger when Jesus faced hunger during Jesus' 40 days of fasting; and Jesus overcame death's "hold;" because "God has raised up" Jesus out of the dead, "having loosed the pains of Death, because it was **not possible** that He should be held under him [Death]." Jesus now "hold" the key of Death (Revelation 1:18); therefore, Death must now give up all the dead.

[672] Hell is a "she;" her soul can be enlarged; there appears to be no limit as to how wide she can open her mouth as she receives those who descend into her (See Isaiah 5:14). Thus, all the dead who were in her shall be "given up" for judgment.

[673] The holding places of the dead who are **not** in Christ—the sea, Death, Hell

[674] This statement implies that some may be found in the Book of Life at the eternal judgment.

[675] Is being cast into the like of fire also associated with the Jesus baptizing with fire as implied in Matthew 3:11-12? That is, the baptism of fire may be referring to the chaff that burns with unquenchable fire. In other words, the baptism of fire may have positive and negative impact. I remember Dr. Clarice Fluitt stating that the same fire that heats your house can also burn down your house [if the fire is not

CHAPTER 21

1 And **I-perceived** a new heaven and a new earth; for the first heaven and the first earth were passed away;[676] and there was no more sea.[677]

2 And I[678] **perceived** the holy city, New Jerusalem, coming down[679] from God out of heaven,[680] **internally-prepared** as a bride adorned for her husband.

3 And I heard a mega voice out of heaven saying, **be-perceiving,** the tabernacle of God with men, and he will dwell with them, and they shall be his people, and God himself shall be with them, their God.

4 And God shall wipe away all tears from their eyes; and there shall be no more death,[681] neither sorrow, nor crying,

---

managed]. The same Holy Spirit that baptize with fire which purges sin can also baptize with fire in the judgment of the lake of fire that does not quench.

[676] As indicated in 2 Peter 3, righteousness will now dwell in the heavens and earth in lieu of the previous unrighteousness in the elements. Peter stated that current unrighteousness in the heavens will pass away, the current unrighteous elements loosed, the earth and its unrighteous works being burned up will occur when "the day of the Lord 'arrives'). Thus, the function of the New Jerusalem starts at the beginning of the millennium.

[677] I am not sure if this is the literal sea or the sea of humanity. If it's the literal sea, it may make sense to provide more expansive room on the earth for all the living that will continue on the earth from all the ages.

[678] Greek: Ego

[679] The Greek tense is "present active" (comparer Revelation 3:21). This means that the City, the Church was descending when John saw the vision.

[680] The new heaven (Revelation 21:1, also see note above)

[681] Death and Hell will be cast into the lake of fire (the second death) in Revelation 20. The principle of "nor more death" relates to the saints who partook of the first resurrection in the seventh or last trumpet (1 Cor 15:50-54; 1 Thes 4:13-18, Rev 10:6 w/Rev 11:15-19).

neither shall there be any more pain; for the **before-most** things are **gone-from**.

5 And he **sitting** on the throne said, **be-perceiving**, I make all things new. And he said to me, write; for these words are true and **believing**.

6 And he said to me, **it-has-become**. I am Alpha and Omega, the **Beginning**, and the **Finish**.[682] I will give to him that is athirst of the fountain of the water of life freely.

7 He that overcomes[683] **I shall give him these things** [684] all things; and I will be his God, and **he shall be to me, son**.

8 But the **timid**,[685] and unbelieving, and the **stink**, and murderers, and **male-prostitutes**,[686] and **druggists**,[687] and **image-servants**, and all **falsifiers**, shall have their **course**[688] in

---

[682] Because we are in Him, Jesus who is "the Finish;" we do not have to be overly fearful about the "scary" end time teachings that prevail today.

[683] Compare 1 John 5:4-5, the faith that overcomes the world.

[684] The winners "in" and "through" Jesus Christ will be given "all things" that God has for us with regards to our inheritance.

[685] This is the Greek word "deilos" not "phobia." The "timid" appears to be those who allow circumstances to overwhelm them to the point of them doing nothing to move forward in God through faith in God (Matthew 8:26, Mark 4:40).

[686] Men are quick to call women whores. However, do they also see themselves as male whores when they sleep around unmarried or sell themselves to other men?

[687] Or magical arts by potions

[688] "Course" also means "section;" hence the lake of fire and brimstone may be sectioned off with certain areas for certain sins; a section for the timid; a section for the druggist, etc. Or will there be turns taken in the lake as per the list given? This truth should make one adjust his/her life now! In Daniel 12:2 we also learn that there will be some who will be resurrected to "exposure and everlasting contempt."

the lake[689] which burns with fire and **God-sulfur-lightning** which is the second death.[690]

9 And there came one of the seven angels which had the seven bowls full of the seven last plagues, and talked with me, saying, come here, I will show you **the woman,** [691] **the Lamb's bride.**

10 And he carried me away in the **Spirit**[692] to a **mega** and high mountain,[693] and showed me the **holy City,**[694] **Jerusalem,**[695] descending out of heaven from God.

11 Having the glory of God;[696] and her light like to a stone precious, even like a jasper stone, **crystallized.**

---

[689] This is a strong statement: the timid, druggists, and idol servants are listed among those who will be burned in the lake of fire.

[690] Two types of death: death when a person leaves the earth until the resurrection; and the second death (the lake of fire and brimstone)

[691] The "great mystery" of the Church being the wife and bride of Christ (Ephesians 5:32 w/Ephesians 5:22-32)

[692] This is the proper perspective to see the Lamb's Bride. The Church must be seen from the perspective of the Spirit not from the perspective of outward appearance.

[693] Note: In Matthew 5:14b, Jesus called his disciples a city. The phrase literally reads, "A **city** set on a '**mountain**' cannot be hid." Therefore, New Jerusalem is also symbolic of the Church of Jesus Christ. The Church is also called a mountain (Isaiah 2:2). Is this the same view as Ezekiel 40:2?

[694] "Great City" is not found in all the Greek Majority texts, and the Alexandrian texts. "Great city" in this verse is only found in <u>one</u> text.

[695] Abraham and the patriarchs saw this also (Hebrews 11:10).

[696] This can also symbolize a sin-free life (Romans 3:23). Jesus, however, lived a sinless life.

12 And had a wall, mega and high,[697] **having** twelve gates,[698] and at the gates twelve angels,[699] and names[700] written thereon, which are of the twelve tribes of the children of Israel.

13 On the east three gates; on the north three gates; on the south three gates; and on the west three gates.[701]

---

[697] See Songs of Solomon 8:8-10 for the benefits of having a high wall that nothing can scale.

[698] There are twelve gates we use as entrance to worship the Father. According to Ezekiel, we cannot exit through the same gate we enter through, we must go "straightforward" to the next gate to exit (Ezekiel 46:9). The practical application of this is that each experience of our gathering to worship should result in a "straightforward" change in character. If we get stuck in a particular gate (refusing to change), it is the same as staying immature by not traveling the straight path in and through Jesus. According to Dr. Kelley Varner, we are to experience all twelve gates (twelve experiences to maturity). He also taught that there are promotions as we accept the dealings of the Lord in each gate. For example, Reuben, who did not refuse the temptation to defile His father's bed, was superseded by Judah who became a worshipper of God in truth as exemplified ultimately in Jesus. Jesus (Judah) now has the birthright!

[699] Per Ezekiel 40:3, these angels also have a measuring reed by which they measure those who enter the city. According to Acts, those who enter these gates should enter with "respect" (reverence) to God (Acts 5:13-14 w/Acts 5:1-12). These messengers are also the five-fold ministers who preach the gospel of Jesus to bring about change in believers (compare Genesis 32:24-32). See note below for further development.

[700] Each of the names of the twelve tribes of Israel points to a nature the Spirit of Jesus must mature in us. Remember, in Genesis 32:24-32, **the angel wrestled with** Jacob (trickster) until Jacob acknowledged his name (nature), at which time the angel changed his name (nature) to Israel (a prince with God).

[701] See Ezekiel 48:30-34 for the order of the "exits" of the City through the gates named after the 12 tribes of Israel. Remember we are to "exit" in maturity through the gate "straight" across from the gate we enter through as we go through the 12 experiences of maturity.

14 And the wall of the city[702] had twelve foundations,[703] and in them the **twelve** names[704] of the twelve apostles of the Lamb.[705]

15 And he that talked with me had a golden reed to measure the city, and the gates[706] **of-her**, and the wall **of-her**.

---

[702] Remember this "City" is the corporate personification of Jesus' wife and bride (Revelation 19:8; Revelation 21:10).

[703] Foundations are people (1 Corinthians 3:11; Ephesians 2:20, etc.). The Church is built upon the person of Jesus, who is alive forever more, and the persons of apostles and prophets who exist in every age.

[704] The "names" (nature) in the foundations are: Peter-rock, Andrew-manly, James (Zebedee)-trickster (remember Jacob (James) was converted to become Israel (a prince that prevails with God and man), John-favor, Philip-fond of horses (points to strength, stamina, fearlessness), Bartholomew-son of ridged (some apostles may be meant to be rigid), Thomas-twin (the double minded became so single minded that it is believed that he evangelized India), Matthew-gift of God, James (Alpheus)- trickster, Lebbaeus-courageous (also known as Judas-praise, **not** Iscariot), **Simon-hearing (a Palestinian, Jesus redeemed the Palestinians (Canaan) from the curse of Noah);** and Matthias-gift of God

[705] The original 12 apostles (including Judas' replacement) are called the apostles of the Lamb. There were also other apostles after the original 12 apostles: the brothers of the Lord (1 Corinthians 9:5); Paul, Silvanus, and Timothy (in 1 Thessalonians 2:6, the "we ...as apostles of Christ" is referring to Paul, Silvanus, and Timothy in 1 Thessalonians 1:1); Epaphroditrus was an apostle (Philippians 2:25). Apostles and prophets were given in Ephesians 4:11 **until** all of Ephesians 4:12-16 is fulfilled. Hence, apostles and prophets existed then, exist today, will exist when Jesus comes, and will exist in the millennium rule. This can be understood by the five bars that held the boards of the tabernacle together in Holy Place (the present Church age) and in the Holy of Holies (the millennium about to be).

[706] Even though he was to measure the gate, there is not specific measurement given; therefore, there is no measure (limit) to number of people who can authorized to enter through the gates.

16 And the city lays **four-cornered**,[707] and the length is as much as the breadth; and he measured the city[708] with the reed, twelve thousand **stadiums**.[709] The length and the breadth and the height of it are **equal**.[710]

17 And he measured the wall thereof, a hundred forty four cubits, the measure of a man,[711] that is, of the angel.[712]

18 And the **in-building**[713] of the wall of it was jasper; and the city clean gold, like to **clean** glass.

---

[707] This is symbolic of Jesus in His omnipresence, who is present as the "chief cornerstone" at all four corners of New Jerusalem (Ephesians 2:20; 1 Peter 2:6 w/I Peter 2:4-5, I Corinthians 3:11).

[708] The City's perimeter was measured at 12,000 stadia like the perimeter of the City Ezekiel saw. The City Ezekiel saw was measured at 18,000 (4,500+4,500+4,500+4,500=18,000); hence each side of New Jerusalem is 3,000 stadia long (3,000+3,000+3,000+3,000=12,000 stadia); hence the actual cube of New Jerusalem is $3,000^3=27,000$ Stadiums^3

[709] New Jerusalem perimeter is 3,000+3,000+3,000+3,000=12,000 stadia; compare Exodus 32:28, 3,000 died at the hands of Moses and the Levites at the giving of the Law—the Law produced death; Judges 16:27, 3,000 died in the death of Sampson –Jesus in His death dismantled demons; Acts 2:41, 3,000 were saved—Jesus in His resurrection distributed everlasting life. 3,000 is the principle of separation between the holy and the profane as understood in Ezekiel 42:15-20 500 reeds=3,000 cubits. Stadium is also defined as "race," a place of running, and preaching the gospel of Jesus is compared to running in a stadium (Galatians 2:2 w/1 Corinthians 9:24-27).

[710] "Equal" can be interpreted to mean that each person, in their prospective "stadium," is "equal;" no one is better than another in the measure they supply.

[711] Therefore, a symbolic "measure" for a mature "man" is 144 cubits (Ephesians 4:13; Revelation 14:1, etc.).

[712] Ezekiel 40:5; 45:13; Revelation 22:5-9

[713] When we are in Christ, He is more concerned about the internal part of us, hence He builds "in" us— "the kingdom of God is **within**" (Luke 17:21) "Christ **in** us, the hope of glory" (Colossians 1:27) "though our outward man 'decays,' yet the **inward** is renewed day by day" (2 Corinthians 4:16).

19 And the foundations[714] of the wall of the city **systemized** with all manner of precious stones.[715] The first foundation jasper;[716] the second, sapphire; the third, **copper-like**; the fourth, an emerald;[717]

20 The fifth, **sardius-fingernail**;[718] the sixth, sardius;[719] the seventh, **gold-stone**;[720] the eighth, beryl; the ninth, a topaz;[721]

---

[714] The foundations are people—Jesus (1 Corinthians 3:11, Romans 15:20; Ephesians 2:20); apostles and prophets (Ephesians 2:20); foundations are also "doing" Jesus' "sayings" (Luke 6:47-48); love is a foundation (Ephesians 3:17), etc.

[715] Precious stones can be symbolic of God's "donation" to us that causes us to be prosperous and to act intelligently.

[716] Transparent and crystal light (Revelation 21:11)

[717] Beauty of the rainbow and points to God's covenant with His Church (Revelation 4:3)

[718] "Sardius-fingernail" is the idea of the transparency of the fingernail by which the color of blood can be seen. This may point to the principle of the Church being founded in transparency through which the blood of Jesus can be seen in us and upon us to bring salvation to others.

[719] The sixth (the number of man) stone is "sardius" which is associated with the word for "flesh" ("sarx"); and since God's throne is made like "sardius stone," this may point to the perfect man, Jesus, becoming flesh in us. This foundation may also point to God dealing with fleshly ways (Galatians 5:19-24), in order for Jesus to manifest through our flesh (compare John 1:14). There is such a thing as "holy flesh" (Jeremiah 11:15; 2 Corinthians 7:1; 1 Corinthians 7:34).

[720] Gold is symbol of God's glory (the "cherubs of gold" made through Moses are called the "cherubs of glory" in Hebrews 9:5); hence rest (7th) in the glory of God.

[721] This Greek word for "topaz" is used in the Septuagint (LXX) for the Hebrew word "piṭḏāh." No definition is given for "topaz" except that the topaz is a pricy stone that was brought from Cush or Ethiopia (Black) according to Job 28:19. This may point to the foundation of Jesus being laid in the black race as directed by the wise master builder (the Father). God was specific to mention that the gospel was also accepted by an Ethiopian in Acts 8:26-4; especially since some of Christendom erroneously thinks that blacks are cursed and inferior. God did not think of the black race as cursed or inferior, as that He directed Phillip to leave a city-wide revival to go and declare the revelation of Jesus Christ to one black man (an Ethiopian). I must note that Noah did not curse "Ham" (the father of the race

the tenth, a **gold-leek**;[722] the eleventh, a **hyacinth**;[723] the twelfth, an **un-drunk**.[724]

---

of so called "people of color" (Africans, Asians, etc.); instead, he cursed Canaan one of Ham's sons (his own grandchild); and **Jesus overrode Noah's curse by restoring Canaan by making Simon (hearing), the Canaanite (present day Palestinians), one of the original twelve apostles of the Lamb (Mark 3:18; Matthew 10:4).** So, Blacks are not cursed. Topaz is also compared to the **price** of wisdom in Job 28:19; hence this stone can point to the wisdom of Jesus; Jesus who is made unto us wisdom (1 Corinthians 1:17-24; w/1 Corinthians 1:30), and the price He paid for us through His "untraceable" wisdom (Romans 11:32-33)— the price of His blood (Colossians 1:14). This stone may also point to priceless wisdom that is found in the black race (symbolized by this stone being found in "Cush" (black). The Church of Antioch, including, but not limited to the apostle Paul, valued this price of prophetic wisdom and/or teaching wisdom in "Niger" (black). A balance look at this is to also say that according to the book of Genesis, God has indeed given the white race, in general, the gift of expansive thinking as seen in the Industrial Revolution. However, all races must make sure they don't fall into the trap of 1 Corinthians 1:21a. That is, mankind should **not** use the ability of wisdom that God has given us to then reason the existence of God out of our minds and life; and to make a "difference" with regards to race (Romans 10:12; Romans 3:22). **God is and God is the Father of all!**

[722] This can point to us being layered with gold (glory) like an onion of the leek family of plants, no matter what layer you peel back you find gold. This is a person that is layered with God's glory no matter how much they are flayed through testing.

[723] This appears to refer to deliverance from the confusion (11th) of homosexuality as depicted in Greek legend with respect to the hyacinth flowers (See Revelation 9:7 in which the breastplate of the army consists of this hyacinth).

[724] It appears that the last (the 12th) foundation to be established in the Church is to become un-drunk from wine (the wine of illicit sex, wine of anger, and drunkenness from natural wine).

163

21 And the twelve gates twelve pearls;[725] every gate was **out-of** one pearl;[726] and the **plat**[727] of the city was **clean** gold, **as** transparent glass.

22 And **I-perceived** no temple therein; for the Lord God Almighty and the Lamb is the temple[728] **of-her.**

23 And the city had no need of the sun, neither of the moon,[729] to shine; for the **very** glory of God did lighten it[730] and the Lamb the light[731] **of-her.**

24 And the nations[732] shall walk in the light **of-her;**[733] and the kings of the earth do bring their glory and honor **of the nations to Him.**

---

[725] We are the pearls that the merchant (Jesus) sold everything (His death) to buy with His blood; and He was resurrected to reinforce His purchase, giving us His Spirit as a pledge. In other words, Jesus did not save us to make us valuable; He bought us with the price of blood because we are indeed valuable (Matthew 13:45-46).

[726] The principle of "one pearl" can also be understood as us selling all (by doing His commandments) to have the authority to enter the New Jerusalem (Revelation 22:14).

[727] Or "place," "plat," or "flat"

[728] Jesus has abolished any need for building a manmade temple to worship in. He and the Lord God is now the temple. God does not dwell in temple made with hands (Acts 8:48; 1 Kings 8:27, John 4:20-24).

[729] According to Genesis 37-9-10, the sun and the moon can be symbolic of the father and mother ministers (presbytery and "presbytess" (Titus 2:3) ministers).

[730] Compare Ezekiel 43:2; God's glory is able to light the entire earth.

[731] Jesus is the Light and the Light is His Life that Jesus has placed in man (John 1:4).

[732] See Matthew 25:31-32—the saved nation according to the judgment of the Son of Glory.

[733] Matthew 5:14—Jesus' disciple is the light of the world, a city that is set on a mountain.

25 And the gates of it shall not be **locked** at all by day; for there shall be no night there.[734]

26 And they shall bring the glory and honor[735] of the nations into **her that they may enter in.**

27 And there shall in no wise enter into it anything defiled,[736] or **one-making stink,**[737] **or falsehood;**[738] but they which are written in the Lamb's Book of Life.[739]

CHAPTER 22

1 And he showed me a river[740] of water of life, **shining**[741] as crystal, proceeding out of the throne of God[742] and of the Lamb.

---

[734] There is no night there because it is an eternal day (Dr. Kelley Varner).

[735] There will come a time when all the nations will bring their "glory and 'money'" to the Church of Jesus Christ.

[736] Compare Titus 1:15; and according to Jude and Hebrews 12, sexuality as in Sodom and Gomorrah causes defilement and bitterness causes defilement, etc.

[737] Abomination like that which is highly esteemed among men; yet they are adulterous (Luke 16:16 in context of Luke 16:1-18).

[738] "Working abominations" (making of stinks) has to do with worshipping (reverencing) and serving (ministering) to the creation or created things instead of the Creator (Romans 1:25-27).

[739] This simplifies who can enter New Jerusalem, the Church of the living God; those who are written in the Book of Life (compare Revelation 3:5; Hebrews 12:23; Luke 10:20; Philippians 4:3).

[740] According to Jesus, this pure river of water of life is the Holy Spirit—John 7:37-39.

[741] Or radiant, shining, lamp

[742] Dr. Kelley Varner taught that the river of the Holy Spirit flows from three places: 1—the Throne of God and the Lamb (the life of the King, Jesus in us); 2—God's Sanctuary (the priestly function of our Great Priest, Jesus reconciling mankind to God from us (Ezekiel 47)); and 3—the belly (the Spirit water that fills our hunger and thirst for God) (John 7).

2 In the middle of the street of it, and on **both** side of the river,[743] the tree of life, **making** twelve fruits, **giving** her fruit[744] **one each** month; and the leaves of the tree for the **therapy**[745] of the nations.

3 And there shall be no more **up-down**;[746] but the throne of God and of the Lamb[747] shall be in **her**; and his servants shall serve him.

4 And they shall see his face; and his name in their foreheads.[748]

5 And there shall be no night there; and they need no candle, neither light of the sun; for the Lord God gives them light;[749] and **they-shall-be kings into the ages of ages**.

---

[743] The practically of the tree of life located in the middle of the street can be seen as a parkway that has a grassy area and trees running parallel to the road the length of the road. The river was also lined with this tree of life on both sides of the river of water of life, apparently the length of the river.

[744] According to Ezekiel 47:12, the fruit of the Tree of Life is the "firstborn" (Jesus) and the "birthright" that comes with being a "firstborn." Jesus is the preeminent firstborn and there are other firstborns (plural) who produced the birthright fruit of Jesus in their lives each month (compare Hebrews 12:23 where firstborn is plural (firstborns) in the Greek texts). See also Revelation 2:7 for further development.

[745] Also translated as "household"—Matthew 24:5; Luke 12:42; Luke 9:11

[746] We should strive not to walk in a curse. One moment we are "up" and the next moment we are "down." God seeks to make us constant in emotions and spirit.

[747] Because God's and the Lamb's throne is "in her" (New Jerusalem, the Church), no curse has power over us to control us.

[748] God's name written in the forehead is for all believers (Jew and Gentiles).

[749] God's light is so pure and bright that there are no shadows associated with him (James 1:17). There is no darkness where God's light exists.

6 And he said to me, these sayings **believing** and true; and the Lord God of the **spirits of** prophets[750] sent his angel to show to his servants the things which must shortly be done.

7 Be-perceiving, I-am-coming swiftly blessed he that **guards** the sayings of the prophecy of this **booklet.**

8 And I John the one-who-hearing and the one-looking-at these things. And when I heard and saw, I fell down[751] to worship before the feet of the angel[752] which showed me these things.

9 Then says he to me, **stare not;** I am your fellow servant, and of your brethren the prophets[753] and of them which **guard** the sayings of this **booklet**; worship God.

10 And he says to me, seal not[754] the sayings of the prophecy of this **booklet**; for the **season is squeezing.**[755]

---

[750] Compare Romans 1:9 with 1 Corinthians 14:32—is Jesus "the Lord God" of your spirit," or is there another spirit governing you?

[751] Whenever there is a real encounter with the Lord or any of His holy angels or messengers, some tend to "fall" (compare Ezekiel 1:26-28; Acts 9:3-4).

[752] This angel is a prophet (Revelation 22:9); and something similar tend to happen to apostles (Acts 10:25; Acts 14:8-15); and to the prophetic Churches (I Corinthians 14:25); with that said, an apostle, prophet or any saint is **not** to accept worship by/from humans.

[753] This means that all the seven angels with the seven bowls of God's wrath were men; yet they are prophets. This same principle applies for the seven angels of the seven Churches, they are symbolic of men (and one of them was married). The same is true for the seven angels with the seven trumpets, they are prophets.

[754] This is clear that the book of the Revelation of Jesus Christ is not a sealed book, especially since the Lamb of God opened the seven seals. Therefore, we can understand the book of Revelation through the Spirit of God.

[755] The season is joining to the sayings of the prophecy of this book as revealed to the apostle John.

11 He that is unjust, let him be unjust still; and he which is **soiled,** let him be **soiled** still; and he that **do right,** let him be **do right** still; and he that is holy, let him be holy still.[756]

12 And, **be-perceiving, I-coming swiftly;** and my reward with me, to give every man according as his **acts** shall[757] be.

13 I am the First and the Last, the Beginning and the Finish.

14 Blessed the **one-doing** his commandments that they may have **authority** to the tree of life and may enter in through the gates into the city.

15 Outside are-dogs,[758] and **druggists,** and **male-prostitutes,** and murderers, and **image-servants,**[759] and whosoever **friends** and makes **falsehood**.[760]

---

[756] This entire verse (Revelation 22:11) seems to be linked to the preceding verse (Revelation 22:10) concerning the season squeezing prophecy into fulfillment and the verse following concerning Jesus coming swiftly (Revelation 22:12); in other words, there will be a time and season when Jesus will come so swiftly that whatever state you are in, is the state you will be caught in whether unholy or holy.

[757] "Shall" is future tense in the Greek text; hence the emphasis seems to be we will be rewarded according to the work we shall do whenever He comes, not necessarily our past mistakes.

[758] Philippians 4:2 where they are equated to evil actors, and "concision" (mutilators), a word used in 1 Kings 18 (Septuagint (LXX) of the prophets of Baal that mutilated themselves; Psalms 22:16 of the crucifixion of Jesus, Isaiah 56:11 of shepherds that can never have enough.

[759] Behind every idol is a demon (1 Corinthians 10:19-21); so, for example, behind Buddha is a demon; behind the image of the beast in Revelation 13:15 is a spirit demon (Revelation 16:13).

[760] Falsehood (the lie) is worshipping (reverencing) and serving (ministering) to the creation and created things instead of the Creator (Romans 1:25-27).

16 I Jesus have sent mine angel to testify to you these things in the churches.[761] I am the root and the offspring of David,[762] the bright and morning star.[763]

17 And the Spirit and the bride say, **come**. And let him that hears say, come. And let him that is **thirsty** come. And whosoever will,[764] let him take the water of life[765] freely.

18 For I testify to every man that hears the words of the prophecy of this **booklet**, if any man shall add[766] to these things, God shall add to him the plagues that are written in this book.

---

[761] This book of Revelation of Jesus Christ is for the Church made up of Jews and Gentiles. It is not written exclusively for Jews. The Church is not an afterthought of God after most of the Jews rejected Jesus; the Church was/is always His Purpose (Ephesians 1).

[762] This may be a reference to Jesus' right to inherit the throne of David because He is the "seed" of David according to the flesh (Romans 1:3).

[763] Jesus will award this to the conquerors of the Church of Thyatira in Revelation 2.

[764] All have the choice of free will; however, whoever chooses to reject the Son, the Spirit of God, and the Bride (the Church of Jesus Christ) will give account to God (Hebrews 10:29).

[765] The Holy Spirit is the water of life (John 7:37-39); and according to Jesus, if one wants to quench his thirst, one must receive the Holy Spirit that God gives to believers as a separate experience that accompany salvation (Acts 2, Acts 10, Acts 8, Acts 19).

[766] It is reported that the Pope can change Scriptures and that some popes have indeed changed Scriptures. This verse (Revelation 22:18) and Revelation 22:19 makes it clear that no one is to add or take away from the book of Revelation.

19 And if any man shall take away[767] from the words of the book of this prophecy, **may God take away** his **course**[768] out of the **tree** of life, and out of the holy city,[769] and the things which are written[770] in this book.

20 He which testifies these things say, **yes I-am-coming swiftly**. Amen. **Yes, be-you-coming,** Lord Jesus.

21 The grace of our Lord Jesus Christ with all **the saints**. Amen.

---

[767] Some have "taken away" from this book by teaching that this book is not for the Church of today. They have put most of it in the future (i.e., they have placed the "great tribulation" after the so-called rapture). When in fact, the great tribulation happened in the days when John received these revelations from Jesus (the Greek tense for "came" in Revelation 7:14 is present tense in all the Greek texts. That means, the great tribulation happened in the days that John saw these visions).

[768] Course and means section, share, allotment, etc.

[769] Holy City is used both of natural Jerusalem (Matthew 4:5; 27:53) and New Jerusalem (Revelation 21:10; 21:21; 11:2). In context of this Revelation 22 and in keeping with the admonishment of Revelation 22:18-19, it seems to me that the Holy City in this verse is referring to New Jerusalem, the Bride of Christ, which is the Church.

[770] Yes, the Church of Jesus Christ will have "course" in executing the prophecies of the book of Revelation. Psalms 149:9 says that "all the saints have the honor" to "execute ... the judgments written."

REVELATIONS FROM OF OUR LORD JESUS CHRIST

SURELY THERE IS A GOD

The setting was Jamaica, West Indies, I was a boy at the time, and I believe this happened when I was about ten years old (around 1972), but definitely before the age of thirteen (the age at which I came to America to live with my mother in 1975). In Jamaica W.I., at property of my grandparent and great grandparents, as I was walking on a white gravel road from the gate of the property towards the houses, I was transposed to mid-heaven and I heard **within, "surely there is a God."** According to my understanding, this was God, the Father of our Lord Jesus Christ, first revelation to me, introducing Himself **in** me; "because that which may be known of God is manifest **in** them; for God has showed it to them" (Romans 1:19). Then an age 24 (which happens to be a number that relates to the priesthood of God), "when it pleased God," the Father, He "revealed His Son (Jesus) in me." (Galatians 1:15-15). He saved me during April of 1986, in Jacksonville, North Carolina while in the USMC, stationed at Camp Lejeune. That is, I met the Passover Lamb, Jesus, during the Passover season, which I believe is no coincidence. I believe, this was the heavenly Father gracing me with certain indications demonstrating, to me, the surety of the blood of His everlasting covenant, and His eternal salvation given to all believers through Jesus Christ (Hebrews 13:20-21).

RAINING STONES

1986 Okinawa, Japan: I had been saved (became a disciple of Jesus Christ) for about 4 months. At the time I was on a three day fast. I was studying on the office of a prophet (At the time I was not sure why this topic was of interest to me. However, I was drawn to study the office of the prophets). It was the third day of the fast, and I was exhausted from the fast;

because at the time, I was in the United States Marine Corps doing a lot of physical training. On the third day of the fast, I was transfixed between heaven and earth, and I saw in a vision these great stones (boulder-like stones) falling from heaven onto the earth. The earth looked like a desert and parched land. I remember coming out of the vision, as I said to m self, I am not supposed to be here (in the raining stones).

JESUS IN ME

In 1987 after returning from Japan to North Carolina, I remember one day being in our home; and I could physically feel Jesus in my body. I felt Him in me; and I could also see His form as another person in my body. I could feel Him looking through my eyes, I felt him in and through my hands, and I could also feel him walking in my legs. I could see, feel, and understand that Jesus really is in me! *2 Corinthians 6:16b says: "For you are the temple of the living God; as God has said, I* ***will dwell in them,*** *and* ***walk in them;*** *and I will be their God, and they shall be my people."*

THE GREAT EAGLE

Around 1988: In a dream, I saw an exceptionally large great eagle in flight high in the clouds. The color of the eagle was as the flag of the United States of America (beautiful and majestic). As the eagle was flying, I heard the sound of thunder. As I continued to listen, the sounds of the thunders became a voice of thunder. The voice of thunder continued, as I saw the eagle in majestic flight, with its large wings pushing through the heights. As the eagle pushed through the sky in flight, I heard the voice of thunder say, **"Judgment, judgment, judgment..."** As I heard this voice of thunder repeating itself with peals, I saw myself on my face, yet I was on my knees. At that time, I was a son of about two years in the Lord; and thus, at that time, I did not understand the vision (compare Daniel 7:27 last part).

A CROWN OF GLORY

9.21.89: Our second son, Jeshua, was just birthed, and my wife was recovering and resting in her hospital room. An angel of the Lord walked in the hospital room where my wife was resting. The angel of the Lord said to her, **"Behold, I give you a crown of glory that will never fade away."** Our ministry is now named Crown of Glory Ministries.

DAUGHTERS OF JOSEPH

1990: While in prayer one sunny day, I heard the Lord say to me **"you are as Joseph before me"** that I should **"go to engineering school you will be good at it."** He then said to me, **"this is the sign that I have spoken to you; 'your wife is pregnant with a girl.'"** I then responded to the Lord by saying, Joseph did not have any daughters. To which the Lord Jesus replied, **"Joseph is a fruitful 'son,' a fruitful 'son' by a well whose 'daughters' run over the wall."** I immediately went to the Scriptures to see if Joseph had any "daughters." I discovered that the Lord is correct as He always is, which fulfills His Name, "The Word of God" (Revelation 19:11; 19:23). Genesis 49:22, in the King James translation says, *"Joseph is a fruitful **bough**, even a fruitful **bough** by a well; whose **branches** run over the wall."* The same verse translated literally, from the Hebrew, says that *"Joseph is a fruitful 'son,' a fruitful 'son' by a well; whose 'daughters' run over the wall."* My wife was indeed pregnant with our third child at the time; a girl, and Charity was born to us approximately a year later. I also graduated from engineering school as the Lord Jesus encouraged me to do; and my wife and I have many spiritual "daughters" and sons; because, God has fulfilled and is fulfilling His words to me.

CHINA

Early 1990s: I saw two huge projectile (nuclear bombs or apace crafts) appearing to rise manually and deliberately (slow speed) from the land of China. I then saw one of the projectiles rise slowly with smoke emanating from its side.

THE GERMAN WAR EAGLE

Around 1992: I saw an eagle formed of limestone in the parlement of Germany. The eagle emblem, appearing to be etched from stone, tore (freed) itself from the wall of an assembly. The eagle became as a living eagle. This previously etched stone eagle, which I understand to be the German Coat of Arms or the federal eagle, was then seen in the vision, poised and about to take flight from the edge or border of Germany. The flight was a flight of war towards America. I knew it was a flight of war because I heard someone in the assembly spoke the words of war towards America. However, the Chancellor at that time counseled the government not to do it yet.

A DRAGON-A MAN

Around 1992, early one morning, during a season when my wife and I were engaged in intensified prayer. After praying the nigh through, we then laid down to rest, and immediately I was in a vision. I saw a red dragon (Komodo-like); and I was battling against the dragon in the heaven. I wrestled this red dragon out of the sky to the ground. I then descended from the heavenly sphere (My clothes were ripped due to being engaged in an intensified and violent fight with this dragon). As I was descending to investigate the state of the dragon that I threw to the ground; the red dragon jumped up and began to pursue me again into the heaven. In his pursuit of me in the heaven, I turned toward him to fight, and fire came out of my mouth and devoured him. The fire from my mouth was so intense, the dragon fell again to the ground knocked out as if dead; however he was not really dead (The Lord Jesus, Himself, will kill him in the Second Death, the Lake of Fire). As I descended from the heavenly sphere, I saw my wife going towards the unconscious spirit beast to throw on the beast some sort of solid foam. As she was about to do this I called out to her and said, "He is not dead as he may appear." Upon saying this to my wife, the beast regained consciousness and stood up. To my amazement, the red dragon had mutated into an animal-man. His appearance match the description of the second beast (the False Prophet or Antichrist) described in Revelation 13:11. The dragon had mutated into that of a man (unclothed at his upper body at that), but he had two huge horns like a male lamb on his head, with the horns from his temples towards his ears, just as a literal ram. At this sight, the vision ended. **Note:** this "man with ram's horn" in the vision I saw looked like Kenneth Copeland, a popular prophet on television (the main one who popularized the prosperity message) in America and he also represent others with the same false doctrine as he teaches. It is also worthy to note in full disclosure, that because I thought so highly of Copeland it took years before I was convinced of the vision; because before this vision in 1992, four years earlier in 1988, the Lord have said to "do not be a servant of man," concerning Copeland because I would watch is shows often.

RELIGIOUS DEMONS

In the early 1990s while living in North Carolina, my wife and I were attending a ministry. While in building of the ministry, there was a man sitting in front of me; and for some reason the Spirit of Jesus opened my eyes to see the unseen. As I watched this man who was sitting in front of me, I saw a demon under his feet. However, as the people who were gathered at this meeting began to play religious songs more and more in this gathering, I saw the demon traveled from under the man's feet, up to the man's knees (he popped up out of his chair); and then I saw the demon went up to the man's neck and eventually his mouth, as the man began to move and speak in what I call a very "religious" form. Needless to say, I was in shock as I saw what happened. There are many things (actions) that men dub as related to God, or inspired by God; however, some actions in some gatherings are results of the *"religion of [fallen] angels,"* or religion of Baal (Satan) [Matthew 12:24; 12:26, Colossians 2:18]. Compare 1 Kings 18 when Elijah challenged the Baal worshippers and how these prophets of Baal conducted themselves; compare Revelation 18:2.

RELIGION OF ANGELS

In the early 1990s, my wife and I visited a Church up north. While in the Church, the Spirit of the Lord opened my eyes to see the unseen and my ears to hear in the Holy Spirit. I saw a monkey-like demon jump on the back of one person and I saw another monkey like demon across the room jump on the shoulder of another person. I heard these two people speak in what appeared to be Babylonian tongues. I heard one demon saying to the other "go ahead, go ahead;" except they were speaking in a false tongue, yet I could understand what the demons were saying in English. One demon kept inciting the other to "go ahead, go ahead." Not too long after I heard these words and saw the demons, I saw one of the young men whom the monkey-demon was inciting, begin running up and down the aisle in religious and effeminate manner. Most of the assembly then followed this person with other falsely incited religious acts. I observed and received instruction. There are false "religions" developed by man and energized by demons that Colossians 2:18 calls "worshiping (lit., religion) of angels." Speaking in tongues is real and a sign of God's seal by/with the Holy Spirit (Acts 2, Acts 10, 1 Corinthians 14, Ephesians 1:13, Acts 19:1-6). Yet, there is a religious system called "Mystery (secret) Babylon" that sometimes sits on "tongues," misrepresenting the Lord Jesus, the Bridegroom and His Bride (Revelation 17:1; 17:15); compare Revelation 18:2.

TRANSPARENT PILLAR

Around the early 1990s, as my wife and I were studying and praying. I started to share with her concerning the faith of Moses that the Lord was teaching me about. I said to her how Moses endured in faith to even see the unseen. As I said that her, I saw an invisible, yet visible, transparent pillar rise from the floor of the trailer, we were living in at the time, to the ceiling of the trailer. The sight was amazing to me; and we rejoiced at the sight. It is possible to see the invisible. Moses "endured as seeing Him who is invisible" (Hebrews 11:27); Angels saw the invisible God for the first time in the form of baby Jesus (Colossians 1:15, 1 Timothy 3:16). I am also reminded of the scripture: *"Faith is the 'substrate' of things 'expected,' the 'exposure of practices' not seen"* (Hebrews 11:1).

THE SPIRIT OF GREECE AND 9/11

I was in a season of fasting and on the 9th day of the fast in 1992, my body became weak due to the length of the fast. I asked my wife Judy to fix me some soup; and as Judy she was fixing the soup for me a was in a trance. In the trance, I heard a voice say, "The way is being made for the spirit of Greece." I then heard a voice say, "A great tragedy shall happen in America," as I heard the voice speak concerning the tragedy to occur in America, I saw a President Bush standing upon a pile of rubble exactly as he did after 9/11 occur (I must note when I saw the vision President Clinto was the president and as a result I saw President Bush before He became President). I then heard the voice say, "After the tragedy, I will bring forth the Boy Scouts."

THE STONE AGE

Around 1993: The Lord opened my eyes one day as I was praying for a particular sister my wife had won (converted) to the Lord Jesus, but she had turned back from following the Lord fully. As I was praying for her, my eyes were opened and my ears were unstopped (I was immediately in the Spirit); and I saw and heard a voice say, **"Pray for her that she does not get killed by 'the stone-age.'"** I then saw her head get knocked 90 degrees to my left (or perpendicular to her body) with a fast-moving stone. The vision ended.

MY ANGEL

In 1993, during a season of severe testing, the Lord previously asked me to close my business to seek Him. What I thought was to be a short time turned out to be about three to four years of the Lord refining me. I came to the end of myself during this time of testing; and during this time of testing I was overly anxious about provision for my family. As I was praying to God for direction with regards to provision a particular morning, I saw in a vision my angel standing next to me by the door of the trailer we lived in at that time. He was dressed in jeans, boots and with a buckled belt. He was standing and leaning against the wall by the door. As I turned to look at him, he vanished. The angel looked like me (compare Acts 12: 14-15). In the vision, the angel of the Lord also spoke to me that morning concerning my provision.[771] He told me to take one of my power tools and go to the pawn shop. He also said when I get to the door of the shop a man

---

[771] At that time, the Lord instructed me to close my home improvement business to seek him in prayers and studies. In my limited understanding at the time, I though His instruction was only for a month. It turned out I had to endure a wilderness experience for a few years. When He first instructed me, His provision lasted weekly; then His provision began to be only enough for daily use; we eventually got stretched to the point of eating grass broth (Compare Deuteronomy 8:1-7 w/Daniel 4:24-25).

would turn to me immediately and ask me **"How much do you need?"** It happened exactly as the angel said. As soon as my feet crossed the threshold of the pawn shop. A gentleman, who happened to be white, turned to me in a very courteous manner and asked me, **"How much do you need?"** It was delightful to me to see how specific the Lord was in His foreknowledge.

TWO SKULLS

Around March 1993: I saw two hills that were shaped like skulls. I then saw an angel whisk me between the two (2) skulls like a speeding whirling wind. [I understood these two skull-like hills to mean the witness (2) of being crucified in sufferings. Jesus was crucified in a place called Skull (Golgotha)]. I was then found to be outside the trailer with the angel again, as he walked with me and measured around the trailer in which we were living in at the time. He then testified to me that in certain time (I believe he said six months) I would be moving from the trailer. We eventually moved from Jacksonville, North Carolina to Baltimore, Maryland.

THE SIXTH TRUMPET

Around 1993: I frequented the Lord, seeking understanding from the book of Revelation. One night, I meditated all night on Revelation 9:13-20 repeatedly. As I continued to meditated deep into the morning hours, I saw a literal great light radiating from the Bible I was reading repeatedly in meditation. At around 7:00 AM the Holy Spirit (the Spirit of wisdom and revelation) opened the scriptures of Revelation 9:13-20 to me. That Sunday morning I wanted to teach what the Lord revealed to me. However, He told me that I should not teach it then. When I went to Church that morning, one of the elders (Elder Gatewood) said to me that my countenance was very shiny. I knew then that the light I saw coming from the Bible was imparted to my body, spirit, and face. With that said, that Sunday morning, after watching through the night, the Spirit of the Lord revealed to me that the four angels were "internally prepared" to kill 1/3 of humanity, thus they had to be bound. Since they were prepared to kill, they had to be kept bound until the time of their release. The four angels became 100 million horses and horsemen. The "great river Euphrates" is symbolic of the four angels who became the 100 million horsemen "gushing forth" upon the 1/3 of mankind with their three plagues. The four angels were being "loosed" from being four (4) angels and multiplied[772] into their other "constituent" forms of 100,000,000[773] horsemen. These angels can be released for "an hour, a day, a month, a year" as God sees fit. The 6th Bowl in which the great river Euphrates is dried up is a symbol of the plagues of the 100,000,000 horses and horsemen being dried up.

JESUS' UGLINESS-AN ANGELIC ENCOUNTER

One day, while waiting for class to begin, a young man (an angel, Hebrews 13:1) came to me for directions (asking where a printer was located). The man was so disfigured in the face that it was difficult for me to look at him. I was so stunned (compare Isaiah 52:14) at his disfigurement that I did not want to even talk to him. I did not even want to be associated with him. Because of these inner feelings, I began to cry within, holding back the tears without. I felt, in my heart, that I had denied my Lord Jesus. The reason this denial was so disturbing to me was the Lord had vividly taught me about

---

[772] Spirits have the ability to multiply themselves. In 2 Chronicles 18, we learn that "a spirit" multiplied itself and spoke deceptive words through 400 false prophets. In Revelation 16:13, we also learn that the Dragon, a spirit; the beast, a spirit in a person; the false prophet, also a spirit; reproduced themselves "out of their mouth" as frog spirits.

[773] Some versions of Revelation 9:16 indicate "200,000,000"

Jesus' ugliness the night before I met this young man, due to my internal struggles at the time relative to my ugly circumstances. Thus, I fulfilled the Scripture in Isaiah 53:3, *"And we hid as it were our faces from Him...."* Yes, all of **"we"** (us) have denied the Lord's ugliness. All of "we" are sometimes still ashamed of Him. If anyone does not believe that we **all** denied Him (His ugliness), take a look at the pictures of Jesus men and women have on their walls. Some have Him portrayed as a handsome Black man, or a good-looking white man. These pictures deny the true look of Jesus' ugliness. Nonetheless, I did embrace the young man's disfigurement, and I helped him. In helping him, I embraced myself. But the idea that I had denied the Lord's ugliness was painful. My mind flashed back to the Scriptures (I was searching for how Jesus must have felt when men "vacated" His person). I realized He was "a man of sorrows" (Isaiah 53:3; 2 Corinthians 6:10). The young man was an angel sent by God. This is because he was a **stranger** to the school campus. I had not encountered this young man before, and I never saw him again on campus or off campus (compare Hebrews 13:1). He was sent to test and heal my acceptance of Jesus' ugliness. Thus, once I embraced the Messiah's ugliness, I was able to embrace myself and my ugly impoverished circumstances at that time.

WHRE IS THE MAN WITH WRITERS INKHORN

In the mid or late 1990s: I (Judith) saw a short vision. In the vision my husband and I were standing on the shore; and as we looked out, all we could see was a vast ocean. We began to walk out into the middle of the vast ocean; and people started coming to us as we were in the ocean. We began to baptize them one by one, unto Jesus. I then turned to my husband and said, "Donald where is the man with the writer's inkhorn?" Compare Ezekiel 9, Revelation 7 and 1 Corinthians 10:2.

JUDITH'S VISION OF HEAVEN

May 6, 1996: I (my wife Judith) was sleep and got attacked by an evil spirit. I fought off this evil spirit by rebuking it. I said in my sleep, "Jesus has overcome you" and the dark spirit left, and immediately I went into a vision. In this vision I saw Jesus on a white horse with a sword, He ran towards this other army full of horsemen. I noticed Jesus was alone, but the other army had lots of men. As they raced towards one another and fought, I heard the loudest song any one could sing. The song declared, "He has overcome them, He has overcome them, He has overcome them ..." Loudly ringing in my ears. As this part finished God took me upward and I ascended in the air and through the clouds. As I ascended, I heard a song sang loudly, "For He is worthy, for He is worthy." The song was ringing in my ears. I saw heaven and New Jerusalem. It was beautiful. The temple was gold, and the streets were gold. The color of heaven was the color of the rainbow - beautiful. As I looked, it finally dawned on me that I was in heaven. I thought to myself, "this is where we will be, and it had to be where Jesus is." As the vision continued, I felt like I was flying. I thought to myself, "I see why Jesus was able to go through walls and move from point to point in a split second after his resurrection." I continued upward and went through some more clouds. It seemed like I came to an end. At this end there was a mist or cloud. I knew God the Father or Jesus had to be behind there. I thought to myself, "I will finally get to lay at Jesus' feet and see Him in person." After these things, I awoke so elated I woke my husband and told him about the vision.

THE BEAST

It was at the beginning of the year 2000, as I was praying, I heard "the beast will be here in 15 minutes." (This word correspond with the vision I saw in 1992 also concerning 9/11.) I must acknowledge that I really don't understand the full meaning of this. So, this is my personal understanding. After thinking about the words, I heard that evening; years later, in light of 9/11, the statement "15 minutes," as it relates to prophetic years, seem to correspond to the event of 9/11.

Here is my interpretation. In the book of Revelation and Daniel, the Bible depicts beasts as kingdoms, and in the book of Revelation "the false prophet" is also called "another beast." Hence, the beast could refer to a ruling kingdom or a corporate false prophet (a false religion), called "another beast." That is, 9/11 happened approximately one year and nine months (or, 1.75 years) after I heard the words, "the beast will be here in 15 minutes." Why is the one year and nine months (1.75 years) significant, and how does it relate to the beast and the 15 minutes?

Since, 15 minutes is ¼ of an hour; or four (4) ¼ hour equals one (1) hour; then one (1) hour relative to the 1.75 years after I heard the words can be understood this way: the 1.75 is to be expanded to seven (7) years. (4 x 1.75=7). Thus, as indicated earlier, 15 minutes of seven (7) years is 1 year and 9 months from the January 2000 when I heard the words, "the beast will be here in 15 minutes." This would place the 15 "prophetic" minutes to be September 2001, the month 9/11 occurred. The beast then must be part of the corporate false prophet, "the other beast" (Revelation 13:11), which would attack America, 15 minutes after the year 2000 (1 year and 9 months). This beast that attached America was personified in radical Islamist in the event we now call 9/11.

THE GOLDEN EAGLE MADE UP OF PEOPLE

On December 31, 2000—New Year's Eve, The Lord had directed me to merge the Church I was overseeing with another body of believers, for a time. He impressed upon me through the written word by revelation that doing this was as Abraham giving up his only son. I did do the desire of the Father, as he had requested. That night as I sought the father to "make sure" I was hearing correctly; a vision broke through to me. I saw a great eagle standing up with its wings raised for flight in the midst of the building where the Church met (Word Alive Worship Center) I was to merge with. **This eagle was made up of people.** As I looked, I saw one of the wings grew to its full length with feathers (where the feathers were people or saint added to the wing). After the growth of the wing, the eagle began to flap its wing for flight. I then heard a voice say, **"From this place you will take flight to the nations."**

JESUS HIMSELF IN JUDITH

Another time, during the mid-2000s, my wife (Judith) went to speak at a Church. After she spoke what the Lord Jesus gave here to speak, she began to pray for those who desired prayer. There was a sister who came up for prayer. My wife prayed for her, and the Lord freed her from drugs and any demonic activities; and the woman was healed from drugs, permanently. Judith's account though was interesting. My wife said that she saw Jesus walk out of her body, lay hands on the lady, and then walked back into my wife's body. Jesus then said to my wife, remember it is I (Jesus) who is doing the work in you (Colossians 1:27). It follows, this lady never went back to abusing drugs, and she is currently doing the work of the ministry completely healed. This is a manifestation of glory that the Lord wants to show **"in"** and **"through"** His

Church. As it is written in Galatians 2:20a: "I am crucified with Christ, nevertheless I live, yet not I; but Christ lives **in** me."

MYSTERY BABYLON DIVIDED INTO THREE

The mid-2000s: On a Sunday, the Spirit of the Lord Jesus impressed on me to teach that mystery Babylon, the great religious harlot system is fallen and divided into three parts. The Holy Spirit also said through me that Sunday that in order to show that Babylon is fallen and divided into three parts, people shall begin to leave the Babylonian systems and come to the body of believers we shepherd in threes (3s). That following Sunday, at first, only two new people came to the place where the we met as a Church. As I continued to preach, I was giving some serious thought to whether the words, which were previously uttered through me concerning people coming to our meetings in threes (3s) would come true; and that indeed Mystery Babylon is fallen. (I later found out that all the people of our Church were also concerned that I had "missed it.")

However, just before the end of the message on that Sunday, a lone person walked in our Church that made up the third person, as the Holy Spirit had promised that some would come in threes (3s) as a sign that Mystery Babylon was fallen. It gets even better, the following week exactly six new people showed up (again two multiple of threes); the following week nine, plus one showed up. The apparent reason the last batch was nine, plus one, is that the Lord made up for one person who did not remain with us. Babylon, is fallen, is fallen is fallen and divided into three (Revelation 16:17-19).

JUDGMENTS OF THE PRIESTS

On April 25, 2002, the lord woke me up early that morning. I got on my knees to pray; and I saw Jimmy Swaggart[774] and heard his name. I saw what he had accomplished as an evangelist. I then saw what he had become after the exposure of his participation in impure sexuality with prostitutes; and his repetition of the act that he was accused of after he apparently refused discipline by his peers; and how he has become a byword in the land among the saved and unsaved. I then began to pray for him that he would be restored. (I thought that was the reason the Lord brought him to my attention).

However, as I prayed, the Holy Spirit stopped me, my ears dilated and the Holy Spirit said, **"Others, who have done like he has done, will also be exposed."** I then heard Him say; He (the Holy Spirit) will be removing priests from the earth (Acts 5; Ezekiel 9). My presumptuous prayer for him ended. I continued to listen as I saw the Pope, and I sensed that God was about to remove him by death also; as I continued to look, I saw what appeared to be Eli. Then I heard the Scriptures in my ears **"I will do things in your day that will cause the ears of people to tingle"** — again, during this encounter my ears were literally being dilated to hear (I could feel and see the dilation).

It appears that Eli represented the Pope who like Eli did not correct his sons who were priests; therefore, God allowed Eli (a type of the Pope) to die, and God killed Eli's sons (priests). Within two weeks of the vision from the Lord, I heard on the news how a Catholic priest was shot for a situation related to inappropriate sexuality. Another priest hanged himself for

---

[774] Note: I mention his name only because I heard his name specifically in prayer. I have nothing against Jimmy Swaggart; and like most Christians in America, I used to listen to his teaching and singing.

similar reasons. Months later, another priest got killed in prison. Ironically, Pope John Paul II, died three years later in the same month (April) the Lord showed me this vision.

A "PLACED SON"

2.6.05: While on a fast (13 days), the Lord reminded me of a word He tried to speak to me around 1988, in North Carolina. At that time (1988) the voice said, **"I have not called you to be an apostle, pastor, evangelist, teacher [...], but a ...** (I blocked out the rest of His words. At the time I was afraid of what God would speak contrary to what I wanted to be—a prophet)." Seventeen years later, on February 6, 2005, in Maryland, while I was on my knees by the sofa praying, the Lord resumed His discourse again, exactly the way He attempted to speak to me the first time in 1988. He reminded me how He tried to speak to me in 1988 and how I had blocked it out. The voice of the Lord continued exactly as He spoke in 1988, **"I have not called you to be a prophet, an apostle, an evangelist, a pastor or teacher, but a son."**

Six years later, in February 2011, I realized that the Lord was "placing me as a son" (adoption). That is, the fact that he spoke to me and said he called me to be a son is in truth the Father placing me as a son. It appears to me that the goal of God the Father is to "praise" over us His voice that we are his beloved sons and all the glory (esteem) and honor (value) that comes with Him placing us as "sons" is for us to inherit now. Galatians 4:1-7 indicates that through the Lord Jesus, the Son, we (the believers in Christ) have been adopted (placed as sons) in the earth as "heirs" being lords of all.

HAIR LIKE WOOL, WHITE AS SNOW

February 26, 2005: I saw a vision of an elder man. He had white hair and white beard, and he was dresses in a white robe. He had a writer's pen (nail) in his hand. I saw the pen being held up and inspected by elder man. The pen was sharp (pointy) with what appeared to be blood-like ink. I then heard a voice say, that **"John (the beloved apostle) was more honorable than they because he wrote with the nail of a cross."** I then saw myself as a young man with a turban on my head. The aged man with the white hair, the white beard and white robe had tears of blood running down from His eyes. I also saw blood on his robe, yet the robe was pure white. In the vision, I kept observing the aged man with the white robe, white hair, and white beard, with tears like blood in his eyes, as he kept observing the pen. Whether the elder man in the vision represents, the Ancient of days, as described in Daniel 7:6, Revelation 1:14; or whether he represented the beloved John, I do not know (2 Corinthians 12:1-4). With that said, here is some clarity with respect to his tears of blood. One of the basic Hebrew words for "tears" is DMAH [D (ד) M (מ) A (ע) H (ה)] (Jeremiah 9:1); and the Hebrew word picture of DMAH is: "blood" (דמ (DM)) that "comes from" (ה (H)) "the eye" (ע (Ayin)). In Isaiah 8:1 and Job 19:23-24, we can also see that "pens" where also made from iron and/or material that engraved.

READER'S NOTES

READER'S NOTES

READER'S NOTES

READER'S NOTES

READER'S NOTES

READER'S NOTES

SYNOPTIC BIO OF DONALD PEART

Donald Peart is married to Judith Peart. Donald committed his life (though for a short period) while Judith recommitted her life to the Lord Jesus around the summer of 1981 after the pair kept reading the book of John and the book of Revelation. Donald read the entire book of Revelation and became especially interested in Revelation 20:4. Eventually, in April 1986, Donald and Judith permanently recommitted their lives to the Lord Jesus. They have been serving the Lord Jesus since and declaring the well-message of Jesus, the Christ. Over the years, the Lord Jesus has worked various manifestations of signs, wonders, and miracles through them. Below are three examples of the Lord Jesus' involvement in the lives of Donald and Judith.

In 1988, while living in North Carolina, the voice of the Lord spoke to Donald and said, "I have not called you to be an apostle, pastor, evangelist, teacher, but a ...(Donald blocked out the rest of the words the Lord was speaking to Him; because at the time, Donald was afraid God would call him to function in a ministry contrary to what Donald believed he should be functioning as--a prophet)." Approximately seventeen years later, on February 6, 2005, in Maryland, while Donald was on a fast; on the 13th day of the fast, the Lord Jesus resumed the conversation he had with Donald in 1988. As Donald listened, the voice of the Lord continued exactly as He spoke in 1988, "I have not called you to be a prophet, an apostle, an evangelist, a pastor, or teacher, but I have called you to be a son."

In 1990, while in prayer speaking to the heavenly Father about going to university to study engineering, Donald heard the Lord Jesus say to him "you are as Joseph before me; go to engineering school; you will be good at it." The Lord also said to Donald, "this is the sign that I have spoken to you; your wife is pregnant with a girl." Donald responded to the Lord saying, "Joseph did not have any daughters." To which the Lord replied, "Joseph is a fruitful son, a fruitful son by a well whose daughters run over the wall." Donald immediately searched the Scriptures to see if Joseph had any daughters. The Scriptures confirmed that what the Lord spoke to Donald was correct. Genesis 49:22, translated from the Hebrew, states "Joseph is a fruitful son, a fruitful son by a well whose daughters run over the wall." The "sign" the Lord gave to Donald was fulfilled immediately. Judith Peart was already pregnant with their third child; a girl named Charity was born to them according to the time of life. Donald also graduated from engineering school. In addition to their five natural children, they have spiritual "daughters" and "sons " because God is fulfilling His word to them. This was also the second and third time the Lord called Donald a son.

On a day around 1991, Donald became disheartened, and he spoke to the Lord about his circumstances. At the time, he and his wife were experiencing extreme trials after Donald's obedience to the Lord. Donald was instructed to study God's Word exclusively, which turned out to be almost four years of intense study and prayer coupled with a time of consistent acute trials or probe-testing. As Donald sat on the sofa that day reading Genesis 2, the Lord began unveiling to Donald an understanding of Genesis 2 with an understanding he had not heard the elders teach. The Spirit of the Lord began to show Donald the sequence of creation, including the man (Adam), the original serpent, and Mrs. Adam (later called Eve). As the Spirit of Jesus revealed to Donald how the Scriptures in Genesis 2 should be interpreted, his mind began questioning what he was reading and hearing in the Spirit. His mind questioned the revelation of the Holy Spirit due to previous doctrines he learned in church from the elders and commentaries. As Donald questioned the understanding the Spirit of God revealed to him, Donald saw the pages of the Bible he was reading being closed one by one, yet the physical Bible in his lap was still opened to the same pages he was reading. This is when he realized he was seeing a vision. The Lord then said to him, "Do not filter my Word through what the elders have taught you."

As a result of the Lord making Himself know to Donald and Judith throughout the years and providing explicit directions to Donald with regards God's doctrine, Donald and Judith have preached the gospel of Christ as the Lord has taught him; a gospel that is centered on Jesus Christ, the Son of the living God and the bride of Christ. Donald and Judith have written over forty (40) books; and they have distributed books in approximately twenty-nine (29) States in the United States, and other nations such as: Jamaica, Italy, Netherlands, Germany, Mexico, Greenland, Tanzania, Uganda, Trinidad, Philippines, India, Peru, Bahamas, United Kingdom, Canada, South Africa, Ghana, Nigeria, Kenya, Australia, France, Sierra Leon, Pakistan, and Brazil. With that said, the Lord Jesus has also graced Donald Peart to earn diplomas from Baltimore Polytechnic High School, an Associate of Arts degree in Pre-Engineering, a Bachelor of Science degree in Civil Engineering, a Master of Science in Construction Management, and a Doctorate in Theology.

OTHER BOOKS

- Poiema, by Judith Peart
- Wisdom from Above, by Judith Peart
- Procreation, Understanding Sex, and Identity, by Judith Peart
- 100 Nevers, by Judith Peart
- The Shattered and the Healing by Judith Peart
- The Lamb, by Donald Peart
- Jesus' Resurrection, Our Inheritance, by Donald Peart.
- Sexuality (a.k.a. Sex Pleasures) By Donald Peart
- Forgiven 490 Times, by Donald Peart w/Judith Peart!
- The Days of the Seventh Angel, By Donald Peart
- The Torah (The Principle) of Giving, by Donald Peart
- The Time Came, by Donald Peart
- The Last Hour, the First Hour, the Forty-Second Generation, by Donald Peart
- Vision Real, by Donald Peart
- The False Prophet, Alias, Another Beast V1, by Donald Peart
- Son of Man Prophesy Against the false prophet, by Donald Peart
- The Dragon's Tail, the Prophets who Teaches Lies, by Donald Peart
- The Work of Lawlessness Revealed, by Donald Peart
- When the Lord Made the Tempter, by Donald Peart
- Examining Doctrine, Volume 1, by Donald Peart
- Exousia, Your God Given Authority, by Donald Peart
- The Numbers of God, by Donald Peart
- The Completions of the Ages, the Gate, the Door, and the Veil, by Donald Peart
- The Revelation of Jesus Christ, by Donald Peart
- Jude –Translation-Commentary, by Donald Peart
- The Better Resurrection, the Person, the Event, and the Age, by Donald Peart
- Manifestations from Our Lord Jesus Christ by Donald and Judith Peart
- You Exist! (Understanding Your Identity) by Donald Peart
- Donald Peart New Testament Exegesis II
- The New Testament Dr. Donald Peart Exegesis
- The Tree of Life, By Dr. Donald Peart
- The Spirit and Power of John, the Baptist by Dr. Donald Peart
- Is She Married to a Husband? by Donald Peart

- The Ugliest Man God Made by Donald Peart
- Does Answering the Call of God Impact Your Children? by Donald Peart
- Victory Out-of-the Beast-the Harvest of the Earth (a.k.a. the beast) by Donald Peart
- Melchizedek by Donald Peart
- Ezekiel-the House-the City-the Land (Interpreting the Patterns) by Donald Peart
- Butter and Honey, Understanding How to Choose the Good and Refuse Evil by Donald Peart
- Wholly Maturing and Wholly Inheriting, Spirit, Soul, and Body, by Donald Peart
- Angels and the Supernatural, by Donald Peart
- The Prophetic Patters of the Two Witnesses, by Donald Peart
- Born a Second Time (Spirit with the Spirit), by Donald Peart
- The Sweet Incense of Prayer by Donald Peart
- Her Seed vs his Seed (Outlined Notes by Donald Peart)
- Melchizedek Order, the Matured Priesthood (Outlined Notes by Donald Peart)
- The Next One Thousand Years-Before-During-After by Donald Peart

CONTACT INFORMATION

Crown of Glory Ministries
P.O. Box 1041 Randallstown, MD 21133
donaldpeart7@gmail.com